NINA KEEGAN

100 DAYS
WITH GOD

100 Devotionals of Hope That Will Refresh Your Soul

"*100 Days with God* is the product of Nina Keegan's 25 year walk with God. Life is a journey and if you spend 100 days with Nina's devotions, you too will learn the signposts that will lead you back to love. As you spend a day with each section, may God give you insight on how to apply it to your life as well."

—Gordon Robertson
President of The Christian Broadcasting Network

"Never in our lifetimes has there been a greater need for us to seek the Lord and listen for His leading. My friend, Nina Keegan, lives like this, and has created this devotional to encourage us to draw near to the King as well! The answer to our needs is to seek Him with all our hearts, with a determination to follow after Him no matter what. You are going to find this devotional is the road map you have been looking for!"

—Terry Meeuwsen
Co-host of CBN *700 Club* with Pat Robertson
and founder of CBN's Orphan's Promise

"This book will change your life! Nina Keegan is one of the most anointed women I have ever met! She is beautiful inside and out! This book will take you on a real journey with God, and in 100 days you will know Him better than you ever have!"

—Michelle Humphreys
Co-host of *Grace Grace with Nina and Michelle*

Dedication

Apart from God, I am nothing, so, first and foremost I want to dedicate this book to God, with praise and thanksgiving for giving me the eternal blessing of salvation through the power of His Son, my Lord and Savior, Jesus Christ!

Thank you to my wonderful husband, Richard, who made me believe in true love again. I am beyond grateful for your love, encouragement, and support. You have my entire heart. I thank God for you every day!

To my amazing sons, Kyle and Kristopher, and my sweet daughter-in-law, Brittany: I could not be prouder of the amazing and strong individuals you are. I love you all with all my heart and soul. Thank you for always being there for me and teaching me unconditional love. You are God's best gift!

To my precious friend and co-host, Michelle Humphreys: My whole life changed in at least a million different amazing ways the minute God put you in my life! I am so grateful. I love you!

To my wonderful friends and sisters in Christ: Clarice, Jennifer, Jan, Marcia, Susan, Ana, Kristie, Cherene, Terri, Becky, and Andrea— you each have brought so much goodness and love into my life, and I love you all!

Introduction

In the decades since becoming a Christian, I have learned, often the hard way, that anything worth doing, and anyone worth being, will require a journey: a journey of decisions, taken throughout life, that can get easier when we give God our ear.

God's path is ultimately where we want to be, but we, as humans, can often deviate from His path. Staying in tune with His word is the best way to bring light into the darkness of the world. Staying in tune with His word is also the best way to turn despair into hope.

The following is a collection of entries that mean a lot to me. These are instances when God led inspiration in my life. Relatable lessons, that I, myself, had to learn, often the hard way. This is the wisdom of my past, which has provided me with the strength and boldness to conquer my future in God's honor.

When you work to live in obedience with God's plan for your life, what results is the best we can ever hope for as Christians. My hope for this book is that it will be a light for you, it will help you put the word of God on your mind daily, and that it will help you boldly navigate your individual path's obstacles and setbacks. This can be better with God. This can be easier with God. Let's walk together with The Lord for 100 days!

"MY CHILD, LISTEN TO WHAT I SAY, AND TREASURE MY COMMANDS. TUNE YOUR EARS TO WISDOM AND CONCENTRATE ON UNDERSTANDING. CRY OUT FOR INSIGHT, AND ASK FOR UNDERSTANDING. SEARCH FOR THEM AS YOU WOULD FOR SILVER;

SEEK THEM LIKE HIDDEN TREASURES. THEN, YOU WILL
UNDERSTAND WHAT IT MEANS TO FEAR THE LORD,
AND YOU WILL GAIN KNOWLEDGE OF GOD."

PROVERBS 2:1-5

The verses shared in *100 Days with God* are from the New Living
Translation (NLT) version of the Bible.

God's Got This!

I remember when my oldest son, Kyle, left home for a university about a four-hour drive from our home in Houston. I missed him so much, I could hardly handle my emotions. Then, my baby, Kris, chose a college in Pennsylvania, eight states away! How was I going to cope? I was a mess, just thinking about how far he would be from us. The worst-case scenario checklist of all that could go wrong played out like a horror movie in my mind.

The last thing I wanted, however, was for my worries to give doubt to my sons. I remembered Jeremiah 18:6:

> "...AS THE CLAY IS IN THE POTTER'S HAND,
> SO ARE YOU IN MY HAND."

How comforting is that? God had been molding and shaping my sons into the men they would become. I imagined God's wonderful hands — strong, steady, secure, safe — lifting up my sons, holding them and protecting them. He loves my children more than I could even imagine. I reminded myself that God is their Father first, and that He only loans us our kids for a short while.

One of my favorite Bible verses is Isaiah 41:10:

> "DON'T BE AFRAID, FOR I AM WITH YOU.
> DON'T BE DISCOURAGED, FOR I AM YOUR GOD.
> I WILL STRENGTHEN YOU AND HELP YOU.
> I WILL HOLD YOU UP WITH MY VICTORIOUS
> RIGHT HAND."

I realized that God's same hands that were taking care of my sons would help and strengthen me, too!

This is because God's timing is perfect, and our steps are ordered. He knew which colleges my boys would choose before they did, and He knew that I would be able to understand why. God's got this!

Embracing Change

It seems one of the few guarantees we have in this life is that change is inevitable. People and circumstances will always be changing. Sometimes, changes are expected and welcomed, but, most of the time, there is some dread and anxiety about the unknown. We all wish we could write the script ourselves. We want to peek into the future.

However, God does not change! He is our constant, our rock! He is a fortress in times of trouble. His love for us will never change!

We must learn to embrace change. Where would we be without it? Change can be a golden opportunity for us. God knows what He is doing! We may need a gentle nudge, a little coaxing here and there, to get us closer to the person we were created to be. Sometimes, we just need to get pushed out of the nest so we can learn to fly.

We can all look back at times when we were facing major changes in the past, and how differently we see those same situations now. We can see just how necessary those changes were, and that they happened for a very specific reason.

James 1:17 states:

"WHATEVER IS GOOD AND PERFECT IS A GIFT COMING DOWN TO US FROM GOD OUR FATHER, WHO CREATED ALL THE LIGHTS IN THE HEAVENS. HE NEVER CHANGES OR CASTS A SHIFTING SHADOW."

When we are in the midst of uncertainty, and maybe feeling quite uncomfortable with changes going on around us, we can relax with the knowledge that God is right here, walking us through it. He will never change. He is the same God you knew yesterday, you know today, and will know tomorrow. There is no need of ours that He will not meet, and no problem He cannot solve. While change is inevitable, His presence is constant!

His love for us will never change!

Having an Attitude of Gratitude

I am waking up on this glorious morning in my usual way. The new day's sunlight streams through the cracks in the shutters of my bedroom windows, and I can hear the birds singing their cheery early morning songs. Thank You, God, for this fabulous day, and for my wonderful life! I'm up, I'm ready, and making my way to the kitchen and the smell of freshly brewed coffee.

I sometimes joke that a book about my life would be sold in the fiction section, because nobody would believe some of the things I've lived through. However, I would always choose to live my life again in the exact same way, changing only one thing: I would make sure God knew how extremely grateful I am for everything, for every single new and perfect day, and the countless blessings each one of those days — whether peaceful or hectic — contains.

I appreciate every joy, every sorrow, and every pain of a life well-lived. Like water steadily carving its way through rock eventually etches out a river, each valley in my life was designed by God to be a learning exercise. Each valley has provided invaluable experiences that drew me closer to Him. Each peak in my life is a place for Him to share my joys, and to show me His unconditional love.

Ephesians 5:20 states:

> "GIVE THANKS FOR EVERYTHING TO GOD THE FATHER IN THE NAME OF OUR LORD JESUS CHRIST."

We should never miss an opportunity to thank God. How can you not see His greatness in everything and everyone?

What if we were to wake up tomorrow with only the things we thanked God for today? What would there be?

Gratitude unlocks the essence and completeness of life. It turns what we have into all that we need. Being grateful can make sense of chaos and give us divine peace for our souls. Thank You, sweet Father, for this and all the days of my life.

Stopping the Fear and Worry

We tend to get all wrapped up in ourselves when we are faced with tough situations. We try to figure it all out on our own, often forgetting that God is standing right there, waiting to be invited to our pity party so that He can help. Sometimes, we simply forget about Him and go straight to Worry Town. How many problems have you solved by worrying? How many have been made even worse by letting your fear get out of control?

To get a grip on worrying, let's follow God's very own instruction list.

1 Peter 5:7 states:

> "GIVE ALL YOUR WORRIES AND CARES TO GOD,
> FOR HE CARES ABOUT YOU."

It's really a choice we have to make: We simply must learn to trust God. If we do what we can, God will do what we can't. The more we give to Him, the lighter our burdens become.

Philippians 4:6-7 states:

> "DON'T WORRY ABOUT ANYTHING;
> INSTEAD, PRAY ABOUT EVERYTHING. TELL GOD
> WHAT YOU NEED, AND THANK HIM FOR ALL
> HE HAS DONE. THEN YOU WILL EXPERIENCE
> GOD'S PEACE, WHICH EXCEEDS ANYTHING WE CAN
> UNDERSTAND. HIS PEACE WILL GUARD YOUR HEARTS
> AND MINDS AS YOU LIVE IN CHRIST JESUS."

So, what happens next? You will get God's peace, and He will continue to guard your heart and mind, to keep more fears from slipping in unnoticed.

Psalm 86:7 states:

> "I WILL CALL TO YOU WHENEVER I'M IN TROUBLE,
> AND YOU WILL ANSWER ME."

God has provided us with all the tools we need to fight our fears. We must call Him into the game, not leave Him sitting on the bench. We need to stop asking everyone but Him for advice, leaving our precious God as our last resort. Trust Him first!

Forgiveness and Guilt

When we hear the word "forgiveness," we think about others who have hurt us or let us down. But, we also need to look at how our loving, merciful God forgives us, and how many of us also need to forgive ourselves.

We can get bogged down with guilt. Sometimes, we drag all our baggage around, to constantly remind us of our past mistakes and failures.

But, God knows our shortcomings, and He loves us in spite of them. God's truth is that, when we repent, our sins are forgiven, period! That is the end of the story.

Psalm 103:12 shows us:

> "HE HAS REMOVED OUR SINS AS FAR FROM US
> AS THE EAST IS FROM THE WEST."

After God forgives us, when we sincerely ask to be forgiven and turn away from our transgressions, He forgets all our sins. God's love wipes our slate clean. We get a do-over! God knows our hearts and our thoughts, and knows when we are really trying to change.

Harboring unforgiveness can be a tremendous wall that blocks our blessings. When God goes to such a great extent to forgive us, and to forget our past sins, then why can't we also forgive ourselves?

Romans 4:7-8 states:

"OH, WHAT JOY FOR THOSE WHOSE DISOBEDIENCE IS FORGIVEN, WHOSE SINS ARE PUT OUT OF SIGHT. YES, WHAT JOY FOR THOSE WHOSE RECORD THE LORD HAS CLEARED OF SIN."

We need to completely get over our own sins and guilt, just like God has already done. God can turn our mess into a message. Accept His forgiveness, and forgive yourself!

Choosing Your Thoughts Wisely

Do you ever ponder about your own thoughts? Our thoughts are very powerful. As the mind thinks, the man follows.

We have all seen those old cartoon images, where a character has an angel on one shoulder and a devil on the other. Our thoughts come from one of two places: good, loving thoughts come from the Lord, while negative and anxious thoughts come from the enemy.

We can change our thoughts as easily as we can change the TV channel with a remote control. But, we need to train our minds to recognize lies when they pop in our heads. We need to immediately decipher where our thoughts are coming from, so we can change the bad ones before they snowball into real issues. When we think wrong, we believe wrong. When we believe wrong, we act wrong!

If God's word is the truth about our lives, then that's what we should believe, and that's all we should be thinking about. We can replace a negative thought with a positive thought — a thought from God!

2 Corinthians 10:3-5 states:

"WE ARE HUMAN, BUT WE DON'T WAGE WAR AS HUMANS DO. WE USE GOD'S MIGHTY WEAPONS, NOT WORLDLY WEAPONS, TO KNOCK DOWN THE STRONGHOLDS OF HUMAN REASONING AND TO DESTROY FALSE ARGUMENTS. WE DESTROY EVERY PROUD OBSTACLE THAT KEEPS PEOPLE FROM

KNOWING GOD. WE CAPTURE THEIR REBELLIOUS THOUGHTS AND TEACH THEM TO OBEY CHRIST."

If a thought does not line up with what God says about you, cast it down! If you know the truth by knowing the Word, you have a defense, an armor to block those arrows of deception that are constantly being slung at you.

When we are filled with the correct knowledge of God, we can catch ourselves in the act of thinking negatively. I encourage you today to get in agreement with the Lord, for if you will change your thoughts, you will change your life!

Going Through the Tough Times

Many of us are going *through* some pretty tough times right now, or have gone *through* hardships in the past. But, think about it: The phrase "going through" itself implies that our trials are temporary. It means that we are pushing forward, moving on, and there will be a light at the end of the tunnel.

Psalm 34:19 states:

"THE RIGHTEOUS PERSON FACES MANY TROUBLES, BUT THE LORD COMES TO THE RESCUE EACH TIME."

He will deliver us! That's a promise from God!

Putting our problems in God's hands and our trust in His love, we cast our cares into His infinite wisdom. We WILL get *through* it all, exactly as God desires. God does not give us trials, but allows them in our lives to test our faith.

He does not give us anything we are incapable of handling. Our problems are not bigger than God; God is bigger than our problems. We put limits on God every time we try to figure things out on our own.

Think of the story of Job. He was a wealthy family man who loved the Lord. He went through a horrible trial, during which he lost everything: his family, his health, and his wealth. But, through it all, Job never once wavered in his love and trust of God. Because of his faith, God restored everything, and much more, for Job. He came through it better than he could have ever imagined. God found a way when it seemed like there was no other way.

Try seeing your problems from God's viewpoint. Nothing is too hard for Him. Sometimes, just when you are about to give up and all hope seems lost, that is when you will get your breakthrough. God can and will see you *through*!

Seeking God's Wisdom in Everything You Do

Wisdom is such an important thing to have! With God's wisdom in our lives, everything just falls into place. The path seems better lit and easier to follow. With wisdom comes clarity, experience, and knowledge. We can say "yes" to things we may have never considered possible without wisdom.

Wisdom causes us to grow in faith. The Bible tells us to make wise choices, according to the Word of the Lord, which tells me that the Word of the Lord is the book of wisdom. It is knowledge for the taking: We can ask for it, pray for it, and receive it!

I often reflect on how many times God has placed me on a path that seemed wrong for me at the time; however, I would always find out just how right it really was. God is the king of hindsight, always reminding us that He knows best. We need to trust Him no matter what, even when we have no clue why we find ourselves where we are, or for what reason. We can rest assured in the knowledge that the reason is pretty significant to God and His wise plan.

We need to throw caution to the wind and trust the well-executed, wise plan of our almighty God. We must be ready and willing to go where God has planned for us to go next! We have to follow our hearts, and believe that the dreams we have for our lives are dreams that God has wisely given us. Every stop along our path is filled with purpose, and we can enjoy the journey and the gifts of wisdom to be found along the way.

Heavenly Father, we ask You today to fill us with Your wisdom, so that we can make wise choices by following Your Word. Help us stay on the path You have wisely chosen for us!

"IF YOU NEED WISDOM, ASK OUR GENEROUS GOD,
AND HE WILL GIVE IT TO YOU.
HE WILL NOT REBUKE YOU FOR ASKING."

JAMES 1:5

Finding Your Purpose

What is purpose? If you do not yet know what your purpose here on Earth is, keep reading, because you are about to find out.

As Christians, we hear so much about this simple, seven-letter word. But, what does it mean? By definition, "purpose" means an end or a goal that one strives for. Are we each given a specific, highly individualized purpose from God? Is purpose consistent, or is it constantly changing? Some people will spend a lifetime in anguish, trying to figure out the earthly answers to those elusive questions. As humans, we like to complicate everything, but I think it's actually quite simple.

I believe we all have the exact same purpose. So, here it is, the answer you have been waiting for: Our purpose is to love God! That's it! A purpose that is simple, yet magnificent in God's eyes.

We are here to glorify Him, and to love Him unconditionally, unceasingly, and infinitely. We are to show others who He is through us. We are to set examples for others by walking in His love, and living each day as if we are on a highly specialized assignment from God.

Our smallest routine tasks can exemplify His love. Giving someone an encouraging smile, or a compliment, can change their whole day. Even cooking dinner for your family can be filled with purpose. So can being a shoulder to cry on, or the first to say, "I am sorry." Do your work with excellence and without complaining, as if you are working for God. These are all ways in which you can show God how much you love Him.

We need to be thankful every day for the opportunity to love and be loved. Everything we do, day in and day out, without thinking much about, is a chance to live out our purpose here on Earth. When all done in unison, as one body of Christ, these simple things can be the most amazing fulfilled purpose!

> "YOU HAVE BEEN SET APART AS HOLY TO THE
> LORD YOUR GOD, AND HE HAS CHOSEN YOU
> FROM ALL THE NATIONS OF THE EARTH TO BE
> HIS OWN SPECIAL TREASURE."
>
> DEUTERONOMY 14:2

Staying in God's Will

I remember a time when my adorable, crazy Peekapoo dog, Zoe, got into the kitchen garbage and skillfully managed to grab what was left of a red velvet cake. She thought she had just won the lottery. She proudly came over to me, dragging the giant chunk of red cake, and plopped it down at my feet.

I couldn't let her indulge in half a pound of cake, but I felt so awful taking her beloved prize away. She didn't understand why, and lay down, defeated.

This made me think about God, and how He must feel every time He has to take something away from us.

As the Bible states in Jeremiah 29:11:

> "'FOR I KNOW THE PLANS I HAVE FOR YOU,' SAYS THE LORD. 'THEY ARE PLANS FOR GOOD, AND NOT FOR DISASTER, TO GIVE A FUTURE AND A HOPE.'"

God has a plan for our lives: a plan for good, not for evil. His plan is to bless us, yet, sometimes, we cannot understand why we are not getting what we are praying for. God understands our hurts and frustrations when we're not getting our way, but only He knows the plan. I believe He must feel like I did when I had to take the cake away from Zoe.

If we would only start praying and asking God for His will in our lives, for the blessings He wants us to have, we would never be disappointed. I do not want anything in my life that will lead me off the path that He has designed for me.

We should pray that He slams shut the doors that we should not go through, and throws open the doors to the bigger and better things that He has set aside for us.

Enjoying Every Moment

When I was a little girl, I couldn't wait to grow up. If you were anything like me, in your teens and twenties, you were always in a hurry to get to the next great stage in life. Always a race against time! I look at my sons, now grown men, with their own dreams and ambitions. It seems only yesterday they were babies, and I was impatiently waiting for them to sleep through the night.

If we could only rewind a bit and push the replay button. Maybe this time around, we could use the pause button and relax between stages, savor where God had placed us for just a little longer.

Obviously, we can't get back the time we so hastily wished away. We will have to rely on our recollections, and remember to cherish every new and glorious moment from this day forward. We need to pause at every step of this wonderful life, and understand that it is meant for greatness in its own right.

We need to live in the now — the present — right here. Look at where you are: It is exactly where you are supposed to be!

Enjoy this random moment in time, because it is so fleeting. This moment, gone in a flash, is one you will never get back. Pay closer attention to your life. Focus on the task at hand, and what you have to do today.

In Matthew 6:34, it is said:

"SO DON'T WORRY ABOUT TOMORROW, FOR TOMORROW WILL BRING ITS OWN WORRIES. TODAY'S TROUBLE IS ENOUGH FOR TODAY."

In other words, if you are busy thinking about the future, you will miss out on the here and now. The future is coming no matter what, so look around you and bask in the precious speck of time you have today. This moment is where you should be.

May we all never again take a single moment for granted, and enjoy every second of this precious time that God has given us!

Staying Positive

I remember times in my life when my view of the world was extremely negative. Grumbling and complaining were part of my daily routine. I also didn't understand why I was not seeing any of my prayers being answered.

It was not until I changed my thinking and my attitude that I began to see God's influence on my life. I realized that I was holding my own blessings captive by having a negative mindset.

Moses had the tough job of leading the children of Israel through the desert wilderness. They were being led out of slavery and to a wonderful new life, but all they did was complain about the journey. Their negative attitudes were keeping them from the destiny God had in store for them. Because of that, a trip that should have taken just a few weeks took 40 years.

There is no shortage of verses telling us that God will see us through ALL that we face when we trust in and fully rely on Him. James 1:2-3 states:

"DEAR BROTHERS AND SISTERS, WHEN TROUBLES OF ANY KIND COME YOUR WAY, CONSIDER IT AN OPPORTUNITY FOR GREAT JOY. FOR YOU KNOW THAT WHEN YOUR FAITH IS TESTED, YOUR ENDURANCE HAS A CHANCE TO GROW."

This is why you should stay joyful, even during the toughest times. God will always bring you through them, but your attitude will determine how long this will take!

1 Peter 1:7 states:

"THESE TRIALS WILL SHOW THAT YOUR FAITH IS GENUINE. IT IS BEING TESTED AS FIRE TESTS AND PURIFIES GOLD—THOUGH YOUR FAITH IS FAR MORE PRECIOUS THAN MERE GOLD. SO WHEN YOUR FAITH REMAINS STRONG THROUGH MANY TRIALS, IT WILL BRING YOU MUCH PRAISE AND GLORY AND HONOR ON THE DAY WHEN JESUS CHRIST IS REVEALED TO THE WHOLE WORLD."

It's easy to say, "Yay, God!" when everything seems to be going great, but it is how we behave in the "wilderness" that shows the strength of our relationship with Him.

Hebrews 10:36 states:

"PATIENT ENDURANCE IS WHAT YOU NEED NOW, SO THAT YOU WILL CONTINUE TO DO GOD'S WILL. THEN, YOU WILL RECEIVE ALL THAT HE HAS PROMISED."

God gives us clear instructions on how to receive our blessings: by enduring trials patiently!

Philippians 4:8 even tells us exactly where to stay focused:

"AND NOW, DEAR BROTHERS AND SISTERS, ONE FINAL THING. FIX YOUR THOUGHTS ON WHAT IS TRUE, AND HONORABLE, AND RIGHT, AND PURE, AND LOVELY, AND ADMIRABLE. THINK ABOUT THINGS THAT ARE EXCELLENT AND WORTHY OF PRAISE."

Imagine our lives if we could follow those instructions at all times! Stay positive, and stay focused on God. We don't need one more trip around the mountain. Let's instead check out that Promised Land!

God's Summer

When my sons were young, I felt like I was pretty handy, and a darn good fixer mom. I was there to help with the endless homework and studying, and I drove my kids to at least a thousand practices and lessons. I especially remember the endless, crazy commotion during the summers. I anxiously tried to keep them happy and safe, and felt like a lifeguard each and every summer.

But, in February 2010, the unfixable (and unthinkable) happened. My boys' father passed away, after a long, horrible battle with lung and brain cancer. We had been divorced for quite some time, but remained friends. We lived near each other. He was a good dad, and the boys were extremely close to him. I couldn't fix this one, but God showed us that He was there.

Philippians 4:13:

> "FOR I CAN DO EVERYTHING THROUGH CHRIST,
> WHO GIVES ME STRENGTH."

My youngest son, who was 16 at the time, called his golf coach the morning after his dad's death and said that he would play in the varsity tournament that day, as planned. He had been up all night, had not been to any recent practices, and had just lost his dad a few short hours before. Yet, he played, because he said his dad would have wanted him to. That day, on 18 holes, he shot 18 pars — a perfect round! There was not a dry eye among those watching. I remember feeling a little less helpless. I knew I could not do anything to fix this for my boys, but God was already there.

He had shown up that very day, to give us all a glimmer of joy in the midst of our sorrow.

God was, and is, always right where we need Him the most. God helped me help my sons. He is our lifeguard. He possesses armies of angels, an unlimited supply of 100 SPF sunscreen, and a truckload of life jackets! We can rest under God's giant, striped beach umbrella, because His arms are wrapped tightly around us and our kids, and He is holding us close.

Doing the Right Thing: Having Integrity

Proverbs 10:9 states:

> "PEOPLE WITH INTEGRITY WALK SAFELY, BUT THOSE WHO FOLLOW CROOKED PATHS WILL BE EXPOSED."

Integrity: What exactly is it? It's an unequaled quality of being honest. With integrity, you have a strong code of ethics, and abhor corruption. It's not following the crowd, but going against the grain and doing the right thing — even when, or especially when, everyone else is doing the wrong thing. It's never compromising your values and beliefs.

Having integrity means that your moral standards are so true, no one would ever doubt your character. It means that you do not conform to this world if it will cause you to compromise your morals or your faith. You are true to yourself, and to the Lord, and you never back down, regardless of gain or loss.

God is aware of each and every time that you are faced with a question about whether to stay true to your faith or not. He also knows how hard it can be to keep the faith, and keep our tempers in check. Integrity means that, in difficult moments, we serve God instead of our feelings. We can either stand for something, or fall for everything!

I challenge you today to always do the right thing, even when no one else is watching. Take the high road, which leads straight to the blessings of God!

Proverbs 2:6-8 states:

"FOR THE LORD GRANTS WISDOM! FROM HIS MOUTH
COME KNOWLEDGE AND UNDERSTANDING.
HE GRANTS A TREASURE OF COMMON SENSE TO
THE HONEST. HE IS A SHIELD TO THOSE WHO WALK
WITH INTEGRITY. HE GUARDS THE PATHS OF THE JUST
AND PROTECTS THOSE WHO ARE FAITHFUL TO HIM."

Heavenly Father, please help us live and walk in integrity, displaying Your light through ourselves everywhere we go. Help us be an example of what it means to be a Christian.

Happiness Is a Choice

"I'm just not happy anymore!"

I've been thinking about how many times I have heard those words from different people over the years. Happiness is subjective. We are trained to think that our joy comes from having an abundance of comfort, money, and possessions. We are taught that we cannot be happy unless we have what everyone else has. We act like it's someone else's job to make us happy.

However, nobody is in charge of our happiness but ourselves. Yes, happiness is a choice! Every single day in life may not be happy, but there is something to be happy about every day! It's all in the way we view things. Material things cannot cause lasting, meaningful happiness. Eternal happiness only comes from having a close, personal relationship with our loving Creator. He loves you, and wants to bless you every day, if you only ask. Radiant happiness will begin to inhabit your mind the minute you decide it's time to be happy!

We can speak happiness over ourselves, we can declare that we have unspeakable joy in our lives like the scriptures promise us we can have.

1 Peter 1:8 states:

"YOU LOVE HIM EVEN THOUGH YOU HAVE NEVER SEEN HIM. THOUGH YOU DO NOT SEE HIM NOW, YOU TRUST HIM; AND YOU REJOICE WITH A GLORIOUS, INEXPRESSIBLE JOY."

By choosing to be happy, we can start seeing ourselves the way God sees us, and we will start acting accordingly. Solomon, in Ecclesiastes 3:12, says:

"I CONCLUDED THERE IS NOTHING BETTER
THAN TO BE HAPPY AND ENJOY OURSELVES
AS LONG AS WE CAN."

Happiness does not depend upon what you own. You have unique gifts and certain talents that no one else has. By seeking God, you will begin to discover these gifts. In other words: find God, find your bliss! By keeping Him as our primary life source, we can remain focused on the good and stay joyful. Being happy becomes a welcomed habit!

Angels Among Us

A dear friend once told me this story about her 4-year-old niece. The child fell from the second-story window of her home. Her hysterical mother found her tiny, motionless body lying on the concrete driveway where she'd fallen. She was breathing, but unresponsive. The paramedics came and rushed her to the hospital. Tests were done as she remained unconscious and unmoving. As the results came back, the doctors were amazed to see that she had no apparent injuries — not one! No bruising, no head trauma, no internal bleeding. The child had not so much as a scratch on her body after falling twenty feet onto a hard driveway. After 18 hours in the ICU, the girl woke up. The first thing she asked was, "Where is the pretty lady in the white dress that catched me when I falled out of the window?"

How could this be? Was she really caught by an angel?

The little girl was blissfully happy as she described how the pretty lady laid her down and smiled down to her until she fell asleep. She said she was not scared at all, and that she wanted to see the lady again. The doctors confirmed that there was no earthly explanation for what had taken place.

Thinking of this story, I began to research angels in the Bible, to see how they are sent to help people in times of trouble. Hebrews 13:2 states:

"DON'T FORGET TO SHOW HOSPITALITY TO STRANGERS, FOR SOME WHO HAVE DONE THIS HAVE ENTERTAINED ANGELS WITHOUT REALIZING IT."

The scriptures say that there are angels among us, helping us and guiding us each day! Angels can be right here in disguise, walking with us.

Psalm 91:11-12 states:

"FOR HE WILL ORDER HIS ANGELS TO PROTECT YOU WHEREVER YOU GO. THEY WILL HOLD YOU UP WITH THEIR HANDS SO YOU WON'T EVEN HURT YOUR FOOT ON A STONE."

God watches out for us so closely, and loves us so much, that He does not want us to even stub a toe! God has legions of angels that He commands to help us. They are continuously standing guard — brilliant, robust, and amazingly strong — ready to move on our behalf at the very utterance of God.

Heavenly Father, thank You for sending Your angels to us. Help us to treat others always in a way that will make You proud, never knowing when we may be entertaining one of Your angels.

Taking Responsibility for Your Actions

Children who are never made to take responsibility for their own actions when they are young will grow up to be adults who never own up to their mistakes, either. These people never get to fully enjoy their lives, because they spend their time blaming others and feeling sorry for themselves.

Every mistake we fail to address is one we will never learn from. Precious lessons about life are learned through humbling ourselves.

James 4:10 states:

> "HUMBLE YOURSELVES BEFORE THE LORD
> AND HE WILL LIFT YOU UP IN HONOR."

I think that society as a whole today tends to have real issues with taking responsibility for our actions. For some people, concocting the perfect excuse is an art form. But, there is more freedom in being able to say, "I messed up, It's all my fault, I take full responsibility and will remedy the situation," than in coming up with the perfect excuse.

Romans 14:12 states:

> "EACH OF US WILL GIVE A PERSONAL
> ACCOUNT TO GOD."

You can either be accountable now, or be held accountable at the gates of Heaven. Live a life of integrity while you have the chance.

Proverbs 28:13 tells us:

"PEOPLE WHO CONCEAL THEIR SINS WILL
NOT PROSPER, BUT IF THEY CONFESS AND
TURN FROM THEM, THEY WILL RECEIVE MERCY."

Heavenly Father, help us humble ourselves before You daily, and take responsibility for our actions. Thank You for allowing us forgiveness while we are changing our ways!

Cherishing Your Friendships

I've been thinking recently about a friend I've had almost my entire life. We met in kindergarten: a couple of 5-year-olds who began a friendship that is still priceless to me today. We have been through it all together, good and bad. I remember getting in trouble in elementary school for calling boys on the phone in the teacher's lounge. I also remember us cheerleading, having summer jobs, boyfriend woes, and taking French Club trips to Europe. We have been there for each other during all the important events in each other's lives: graduations, bridal and baby showers, weddings, new babies, divorce, and moving away. She is also my oldest son's godmother. Whenever we talk, we laugh about ridiculous things that no one else but us would understand.

It occurred to me how rare it is today, to have a friend in your life for so long; someone who knows you better than anyone else ever could. It's like family that you got to choose yourself!

Friends are like little gems that the Lord doles out to us because He loves to see us happy! How truly blessed we all are to have dear friends in our lives.

A friend knows you completely, inside and out. A friend understands where you have been, knows where you are going, and loves you in spite of all your flaws. A beloved friend is someone who walks in when all others walk out.

Proverbs 17:17 states:

"A FRIEND IS ALWAYS LOYAL, AND A BROTHER
IS BORN TO HELP IN TIME OF NEED."

We need to take care of our friendships and never let the ball drop. It's never too late to rekindle a neglected friendship. I truly believe that, when an old friend's name suddenly crosses your mind out of the blue, it's God's way of saying, "This is My gift to you."

Proverbs 18:24 tells us:

"THERE ARE 'FRIENDS' WHO DESTROY EACH OTHER,
BUT A REAL FRIEND STICKS CLOSER THAN A BROTHER."

Heavenly Father, thank You for all the wonderful friends You put in my life!

Doing It Afraid

Some friends of mine were recently telling me about how they had gone skydiving because it was on their "bucket list." I asked them if they would ever do it again, and the response was overwhelmingly, "No way, it was terrifying!"

So, I got thinking to about this, and asked a few other people what they have at the top of their bucket lists. They mentioned adventurous things that people would generally be extremely fearful of, like climbing Mount Everest, swimming with sharks, or driving a professional race car at top speed on the Indy 500 track.

Why do we put our fears on to a "to-do" list that we will probably never get around to doing? Don't we kind of do that in our daily lives with all our fears, even the minor ones?

Fears are nothing more than obstacles that stand in the way of progress. They cannot be conquered until we make up our minds to conquer them!

Romans 8:37 tells us:

> "...OVERWHELMING VICTORY IS OURS
> THROUGH CHRIST, WHO LOVED US."

God's perfect love casts out all fears. When we let Him into our hearts, He begins tearing down our walls of fear, brick by brick. The walls begin to slowly erode, until we finally trust Him at all times.

Isaiah 41:10 states:

> "DON'T BE AFRAID, FOR I AM WITH YOU. DON'T
> BE DISCOURAGED, FOR I AM YOUR GOD. I WILL

STRENGTHEN YOU AND HELP YOU. I WILL HOLD
YOU UP WITH MY VICTORIOUS RIGHT HAND."

God will hold your hand when you need encouragement. You don't need to do it afraid, because you know that God is right there to catch you when you fall. You need only call His name and be rescued.

Heavenly Father, we can live our lives free from fear knowing You are with us, guiding and protecting us each and every single day.

Does Everyone Really Win?

"Everyone is a winner!" This seems to be the mantra of children's sports today. Whether you were the talented MVP of the team, or you missed practice and displayed a negative attitude, you receive a glorious, shiny trophy. The problem with this theme in society these days, despite some people thinking that this sounds kind of harsh, is that it is unfair and harmful to let everyone win at everything all the time.

By giving everyone a trophy, we create a world where people feel like they never have to work hard to achieve success. They have no way to learn how to plan, think, problem solve, or achieve something based on their own merits. They are cheated of the satisfaction of the payoff you get for a strong effort. You can't ever fully appreciate success in life without having experienced failure.

We must learn for ourselves, so that we can teach our children, that hard work and determination always pays off. Learn what it means to achieve, persevere, and accomplish.

Proverbs 10:4 states:

> "LAZY PEOPLE ARE SOON POOR;
> HARD WORKERS GET RICH."

If you want something bad enough, you can make it happen for yourself. If you will do what you can, God will do what you can't.

The conflicts we encounter on the road to success are benefits to us in the long run. We learn perseverance through struggle. Through trial and error, we learn to adapt ourselves to new situations. There is a monumental difference between failing and not trying. So, never give up!

Heavenly Father, help us work hard to follow our own dreams and goals, and to always give our all. Help us stay focused on You as we strive for excellence.

Love Letters From God

How does our glorious Heavenly Father communicate with each and every one of us? He only requires us to have our minds and our hearts open and ready, to hear Him when we pray.

Our hectic, self-centered lives can keep us more focused on our to-do lists than on our loving God. Prayer time can be rushed. Sure, we take the time to pour it all out, to spill our guts and make requests. Sometimes, we rival a child's Christmas wish-list. We don't skip a beat as we pray. We barely come up for air. "God, please change my circumstances. Can you help me worry less, or work more? Would you please?" And then, we look at the clock, and decide we have to rush to the next item on the list, and prayer time is over!

It's like we invite God over for morning tea, but send Him out the door before He even sits at the table!

We leave Him hanging, not letting Him get a word in edgewise. We are supposed to be in a relationship with Him, which requires both talking and listening.

Jeremiah 7:23 states:

> "...OBEY ME, AND I WILL BE YOUR GOD, AND YOU WILL BE MY PEOPLE. DO EVERYTHING AS I SAY, AND ALL WILL BE WELL!"

God also communicates to us through His written word. You may be reading the Bible when a verse seems to leap off the page, dealing with the very concerns you are presently worried about.

I think of these little supernatural winks from God as personalized love letters from Him. The more we get to know the Bible, and study and rely on God's Word, the more of God's sweet love letters we will receive.

Start spending meaningful, uninterrupted, quality prayer time with God. Give Him time to talk and to move in you as you sit patiently and silently. Learn to recognize His voice. Cherish your sweet love letters. Never miss out on your daily cup of tea with God!

Doing One Thing

I will never forget a crazed, rushed morning from a few years ago. I was in a long line at the coffee shop for my much-needed morning cup of joe. Finally, I got to order my latte. As I handed the cashier money, she smiled at me and said, "A man gave me one hundred dollars and told me to buy coffee for all the people in line until it's spent. So, your coffee is free today!" Imagine what a wonderful surprise this was: a blessing of kindness in the midst of my stressful morning!

I thought about the gentleman that purchased our coffees. He was probably every bit as hurried to get to work as the rest of us, but he took a few extra seconds to bless some people he didn't even know. He would get no thanks, just a great feeling of happiness from doing such a deed.

I think that, too often in our busy and hurried lives, we greatly underestimate the power of a kind word, a cheerful smile, a heartfelt compliment, or a simple, random act of kindness.

Acts 20:35 tells us:

> "AND I HAVE BEEN A CONSTANT EXAMPLE OF HOW YOU CAN HELP THOSE IN NEED BY WORKING HARD. YOU SHOULD REMEMBER THE WORDS OF THE LORD JESUS: 'IT IS MORE BLESSED TO GIVE THAN TO RECEIVE.'"

A trickle of kindness can turn into a stream, a stream into a river, and a river into a flood of kindness that spills over into a massive ocean of people who all pay it forward, an ocean that extends out across the borders of hatred, and spreads blessings until kindness is a certainty, rather than an occasional rarity.

Colossians 3:12 states:

"SINCE GOD CHOSE YOU TO BE THE HOLY PEOPLE HE LOVES, YOU MUST CLOTHE YOURSELVES WITH TENDERHEARTED MERCY, KINDNESS, HUMILITY, GENTLENESS, AND PATIENCE."

Heavenly Father, we thank You for leading us to be a blessing to others today. We thank You for your gentle nudges to throw kindness around like confetti!

Having Balance in Your Life

Are you one of those people that always seems to be scrambling, always worrying about not having enough time in the day to do it all? Many of us routinely feel as if we are being pulled in a million different directions. Sooner or later, this "multitasking" can have some serious repercussions on our lives and our well-being. Something's got to give!

We need to have some balance in our lives. Having balance will help us regain control and enjoy life, instead of continually stressing over it.

Many of you are probably thinking that this all sounds good on paper, but there is nothing you can possibly change. But, when we are spread too thin, we must give ourselves a break, and take some time to rejuvenate and rest. Schedule time for yourself and God first; then, you will be a better you for everyone and everything else.

Matthew 6:33 tells us:

> "SEEK THE KINGDOM OF GOD ABOVE ALL ELSE,
> AND LIVE RIGHTEOUSLY, AND HE WILL GIVE YOU
> EVERYTHING YOU NEED."

When you spend some quality time with God each day, meditating on Him and His words, it will give you the grace you need to make it through the day joyfully, stress-free, and well-equipped for anything that comes your way.

Think of Mary and Martha. When Jesus arrived at their home, Martha continued with her busy tasks, but Mary stopped what she was doing and sat at Jesus' feet to spend time with Him. There is a time for work, and a time to sit at God's feet and soak up His rejuvenating strength. We must find the right balance.

Heavenly Father, please help me stay balanced in my life by focusing on You first, and letting You be my guide.

Riding Out the Storm

We have taken many family vacations to the beautiful Caribbean island of Roatán. It has an extraordinarily tranquil vibe to it. It is surrounded by turquoise waters, and blanketed in lush vegetation, with jungle-covered mountains. The people living there seem as though they do not have a care in the world. They are laid back and happy.

One time, we spent our vacation watching the locals preparing for the arrival of Hurricane Ernesto. The weather updates predicted that the storm was heading straight towards Roatán!

Having lived in Houston for years, I am certainly no stranger to hurricanes. These storms can be devastating. The constantly streaming news media always hypes up the storm, and we prepare in a panic.

This time, it was different. On Roatán, there was an overwhelming sense of calm. No one seemed panicked about this fury about to be unleashed upon them! People stayed focused and steadily worked together.

The sense of ease they walk in on a daily basis did not change when they were faced with unexpected adversity. They literally rode the storm out.

The Bible says, in Exodus 14:13-14:

> "DON'T BE AFRAID. JUST STAND STILL AND WATCH THE LORD RESCUE YOU TODAY. THE LORD HIMSELF WILL FIGHT FOR YOU. JUST STAY CALM."

We, as Christians, should be able to stay calm and trust God through all the proverbial storms we face in our lives. We may not have a choice about the storms we find ourselves in, but we can choose how we weather them.

Proverbs 1:33 states:

"...ALL WHO LISTEN TO ME WILL LIVE IN PEACE, UNTROUBLED BY FEAR OF HARM."

Promises do not get any better than that! We can live in complete safety. We can remain at ease, if we just listen to God. He can and will carry us through it all. There is no hurricane that can defeat the love of God!

Unclaimed Blessings

Are you still taking baby steps on your walk through Christianity? We can all easily say the prayer of salvation and receive Jesus as our Lord and Savior. Then what? What's next?

Unfortunately, many remain immature in their Christianity for their entire lives, and never fully experience all of God's best. They fail to realize that the prayer of salvation comes with a large instruction manual: the Bible.

I once read a story that said that, after we go through Heaven's pearly gates, each of us will find a box with our name etched on the front. The box will be filled to the brim with all of the unused blessings that the Lord had wanted each one of us to receive here on Earth.

If this is true, then how can we grow into mature Christians, so that we can receive the blessings that are stored for us? I'm sure that you, like me, would like nothing more than to arrive in Heaven and find a completely empty box, because you had already received every single remarkable gift God had meant for you. The only way to achieve this is by faith, faith, and more faith!

Psalm 106:3 states:

"THERE IS JOY FOR THOSE WHO DEAL JUSTLY WITH OTHERS, AND ALWAYS DO WHAT IS RIGHT."

Start by studying and learning the word of God. You will begin to see blessing after astonishing blessing come your way as you receive the grace that God has in store for you.

Psalm 21:6 tells us:

"YOU HAVE ENDOWED HIM WITH ETERNAL BLESSINGS
AND GIVEN HIM THE JOY OF YOUR PRESENCE."

Heavenly Father, we long to become mature Christians by growing in our faith. We want to be a blessing to others as You transform us from glory to glory.

Are You Praying or Complaining?

We all know a certain type of people, who are never happy and have a string of complaints long enough to circle the globe a few dozen times. When you recognize them on the street, or see their phone number pop up on your caller ID, your heart just sinks. You certainly don't want them putting any more rotten apples into your shiny new apple cart!

Well, it was probably not by accident that you were put in these people's paths at the moment you were. Maybe God is trying to use you as a blessing to someone else. We need to unselfishly lend an ear, and give ourselves over to the work God wants us to do.

I Peter 4:10 states:

> "GOD HAS GIVEN EACH OF YOU A GIFT FROM
> HIS GREAT VARIETY OF SPIRITUAL GIFTS.
> USE THEM WELL TO SERVE ONE ANOTHER."

There are times when we've all fallen victim to a negative mindset. Why would Christians ever complain, when we can have, be, and experience God's best? It starts with the choices we, as individuals, make each day. Think about it. When you go before God in prayer, are you praying, or complaining? Are you whining that your neighbors seem so blessed, while explaining to God that they are not as good Christians as you are? If so, then you need to stop telling your Creator how to do His job, and start focusing on the many wonderful blessings you do have.

You need to decide, right now, that you will be happy today, tomorrow, and every day of your life, because you realize the miraculous blessing of having a savior, Jesus! Let's praise God for salvation: the ultimate blessing!

Thank You, Father, as we take time today to count our blessings. Let us never miss a chance to bless someone through You, and may we continually have grateful hearts, regardless of our circumstances!

Seasons of Change

What is it about a simple change in weather that can bring out the best in people? Each new season feels like the blessing of a fresh start.

The Bible also uses seasons to reference new beginnings in our lives. Seasons are metaphors for God's perfect timing in delivering us through all the changes He makes in our lives. If we are obedient in following Him, even if we do not fully understand or welcome the changes, we will reap blessings during the right season.

Galatians 6:9 states:

> "SO LET'S NOT GET TIRED OF DOING WHAT IS GOOD.
> AT JUST THE RIGHT TIME WE WILL REAP A HARVEST
> OF BLESSING IF WE DON'T GIVE UP."

A beautiful tree with lush, green foliage and beautiful, ripe fruit offers shelter, nourishment, and shade, but only temporarily. Then, the leaves turn brilliant hues of red, gold, and orange, offering us a wonderful spectacle to behold, artfully painted with God's brushstrokes. Then, those leaves must fall, leaving the tree bare and vulnerable as it survives through the harshest of seasons. The tree must go through winter to begin its new life, a new cycle, which debuts with buds and fragrant blossoms.

No matter how long and strenuous our trials seem, there is always another season ahead, a season of new beginnings.

Psalm 1:3 states:

"THEY ARE LIKE TREES PLANTED ALONG THE
RIVERBANK, BEARING FRUIT EACH SEASON.
THEIR LEAVES NEVER WITHER, AND THEY
PROSPER IN ALL THEY DO."

We can stay firmly planted in faith so that we will never wither,
but instead prosper and produce good fruit. Only when we have
learned all there is to learn in this season will God move us to the
next, more bountiful season.

If God Emailed Us

If God could send us an email, what do you think He would say to us? Perhaps you can imagine with me for a moment that it would be something like this:

"My dearest sweet children,

Oh, how I love you all! I love watching over you each and every day. I share every moment. You are My children, and I do not want to miss a thing.

Many of you ask why I seem so distant. Please, don't think even for a moment that I am not right by your side. When you are racing through traffic, I am in the passenger seat, keeping you safe. That was Me who kept your child from getting hurt on the playground. I was that random person who paid you a compliment and made you smile. I am the soft breeze you feel on your cheek every morning when you drink your coffee on the back porch. I am always right there.

It makes Me sad when I see you hurting, angry, jealous, or feeling sorry for your-selves. That is not My plan for you. I want to relieve you of all of these sufferings, but I can only be what you invite Me to be.

I am not a pushy God; you need to choose Me first. Invite Me in! I long to perfect all that concerns you. I will meet you right where you are. Nothing you have done can make Me love you less.

Together, we can make this world a better place. People will see your light and your salvation. They will notice My presence in you, and long to live in that same peace.

Do not forget Me. I am everywhere you are. Call to Me! You are like precious jewels to Me. My beautiful children!

Your Heavenly Father,

God"

"AND I AM CONVINCED THAT NOTHING CAN EVER
SEPARATE US FROM GOD'S LOVE. NEITHER DEATH
NOR LIFE, NEITHER ANGELS NOR DEMONS, NEITHER
OUR FEARS FOR TODAY NOR OUR WORRIES ABOUT
TOMORROW — NOT EVEN THE POWERS OF HELL CAN
SEPARATE US FROM GOD'S LOVE."

ROMANS 8:38

Being Yourself

Imagine if I described to you a beautiful mountainside meadow, covered in wildly blooming flowers on a perfect sunny day. Now, if I were to ask all of you to sit down with a sketch pad and draw the scene you saw in your minds, what would your drawings look like? If we were to hang them, side by side, in a beautiful art gallery, I bet you that no two would be alike, or even close!

Our visions are all unique. God has made each of us to be an unparalleled individual. The Bible says that He has drawn each of us; we are His artwork! Each of us has talents and gifts that we share with no other soul on this planet.

Jeremiah 31:3 states:

> "LONG AGO THE LORD SAID TO ISRAEL:
> 'I HAVE LOVED YOU, MY PEOPLE, WITH
> AN EVERLASTING LOVE. WITH UNFAILING LOVE
> I HAVE DRAWN YOU TO MYSELF.'"

If we can grasp the concept that we are not ever meant to be just like anyone else, we can stop wishing to be different. We spend so much time trying to be something we're not that we miss out on being the unique and wonderfully made human beings that God designed us to be! When we compare ourselves to others, we are basically telling God that He did not do a good enough job with us.

Ephesians 2:10 states:

"FOR WE ARE GOD'S MASTERPIECE. HE HAS CREATED US ANEW IN CHRIST JESUS, SO WE CAN DO THE GOOD THINGS HE PLANNED FOR US LONG AGO."

Be who you are meant to be! You are a complete package, all tied up with God's ribbons and sealed with His mighty stamp of approval. You are exactly who you are, for reasons and purposes that only God knows. So, go paint that picture in your mind exactly how you see it!

Simple Abundance

I often remember a trip I took to Scotland, to a town that looked like time had forgotten it. The hand-carved architecture and cobblestone streets were not mixed with shopping malls or billboards. People could walk to the small, family-owned shops to buy their produce, bread, and cheese. They seemed wonderfully happy. The absolute definition of simple abundance!

Matthew 6:24 tells us:

> "NO ONE CAN SERVE TWO MASTERS. FOR YOU WILL HATE ONE AND LOVE THE OTHER; YOU WILL BE DEVOTED TO ONE AND DESPISE THE OTHER. YOU CANNOT SERVE GOD AND BE ENSLAVED TO MONEY."

We often idolize stuff we own, but, when something breaks, we toss it and hurry to buy a brand new product. We buy bigger and better things. We wait in line for the latest and the greatest product. We accumulate way more than we need, or can even use. It is like a bottomless pit! We are, it seems, trying to fill a void that only God can fill.

Luke 12:34 states:

> "WHEREVER YOUR TREASURE IS, THERE THE DESIRES OF YOUR HEART WILL ALSO BE."

When we let go of the complexity of having and maintaining all of our stuff, we can concentrate on what is really important. We get overwhelmed and tired from keeping up with the Joneses.

We need to take action, to let go of the things that are bogging us down.

Matthew 16:26 asks:

"AND WHAT DO YOU BENEFIT IF YOU GAIN THE WHOLE WORLD BUT LOSE YOUR OWN SOUL? IS ANYTHING WORTH MORE THAN YOUR SOUL?"

Life is brief, and we need to simplify it and enjoy the little things. Take time to smell the roses. Be present in your own life.

Heavenly Father, help us redirect our focus to You and realize what's important, as we weed out materialism and instead enjoy Your simple abundance!

God Is Our Strong Tower

Do you ever feel that every day is an uphill battle? Does it feel that, just when you are gaining some ground, you slip? Or, does it seem like it is always one step forward and three steps back?

If so, it is likely that you get overwhelmed and frustrated, and you feel like giving up. You often ask yourself where God is. Why does He seem so far away?

Psalm 31:14-15 tells us:

"BUT I AM TRUSTING YOU, O LORD, SAYING, "YOU ARE MY GOD!" MY FUTURE IS IN YOUR HANDS. RESCUE ME FROM THOSE WHO HUNT ME DOWN RELENTLESSLY."

God is never far from us. Our good and bad times are in His hands. He is always right there, on standby, waiting for you to call His name. I am sure there have been times in all of our lives when we felt like God was not answering our prayers. But, today, if we look back, we can see that we were wrong. God was looking out for us. Once we realize this, we know we would not change a thing in our pasts!

Sometimes, life feels like a slick road; we feel like we have no traction, and our lives are aimlessly spinning out of control. But, God is ALWAYS in control of our lives.

Psalm 18:2-3 states:

"THE LORD IS MY ROCK, MY FORTRESS, AND MY SAVIOR; MY GOD IS MY ROCK, IN WHOM I FIND PROTECTION. HE IS MY SHIELD, THE POWER THAT

SAVES ME, AND MY PLACE OF SAFETY. I CALLED ON
THE LORD, WHO IS WORTHY OF PRAISE, AND HE
SAVED ME FROM MY ENEMIES."

Trust the Lord today with everything you are facing. Let Him rain peace down over you, and let His perfect love blanket your concerns.

Heavenly Father, when we are weak, You are strong! Thank You for lifting us up during times of need, as You help us scale our uphill battles with ease.

Stepping Out in Faith

Do you ever look back on a rough time in your life and think, in amazement, how everything miraculously worked out in the end? You know now that God was always there with you, even though you could not see it at the time. Adverse times in our lives are meant to strengthen our relationship with God.

Romans 8:28 tells us:

> "AND WE KNOW THAT GOD CAUSES EVERYTHING TO WORK TOGETHER FOR THE GOOD OF THOSE WHO LOVE GOD AND ARE CALLED ACCORDING TO HIS PURPOSE FOR THEM."

I refer to these times of uncertainty as faith stretchers. When we are at our very lowest, we can finally get out of our own way, to make room for God to help us.

Philippians 4:13 states:

> "FOR I CAN DO EVERYTHING THROUGH CHRIST, WHO GIVES ME STRENGTH."

There are so many messages and lessons learned during our times of struggle. When we realize that we cannot go through these trials on our own — when we commit them to God — we start to see results.

John 14:13-14 states:

"YOU CAN ASK FOR ANYTHING IN MY NAME,
AND I WILL DO IT, SO THAT THE SON CAN BRING
GLORY TO THE FATHER. YES, ASK ME FOR ANYTHING
IN MY NAME, AND I WILL DO IT!"

Sometimes, we need to go through the rough times, and flounder out of our comfort zone, to grow in our faith. Each time we trust God with a problem, we are putting another stepping stone of faith on our path.

Remember, always to step out in faith, and trust in the Lord for all you need, and for anything you are going through!

Overcoming Self-Appointed Limitations

I know many people that just can't seem to get a break, and have a mindset of, "This is as good as it gets."

We can set major limitations in our own lives, and the lives of our families, by thinking this way. We become products of our surroundings. If you grew up in a very unhappy household, chances are, you have carried those habits of limited thinking straight through into your adult life.

I once heard a story about a lady who always made a beautiful ham for holiday dinners. Before she placed it in the oven to cook, she always cut off a slice from each end. One day, her young daughter asked her why she did that. The lady replied that her own mother had always done it that way. She had never thought about it, but asked her mother for the reason the next time they talked. Her mother laughed, and said, "I always used to cut the ends of the ham off because my pan was too small to fit it!"

So, think about it: How many of us cut the ends off the ham, rather than get a larger pan? Sometimes, we don't even question our reality. We never wander out past the walls of our own set limitations.

Romans 5:17 states:

"FOR THE SIN OF THIS ONE MAN, ADAM, CAUSED DEATH TO RULE OVER MANY. BUT EVEN GREATER IS GOD'S WONDERFUL GRACE AND HIS GIFT OF

RIGHTEOUSNESS, FOR ALL WHO RECEIVE IT WILL LIVE IN TRIUMPH OVER SIN AND DEATH THROUGH THIS ONE MAN, JESUS CHRIST."

We have royal blood flowing through our veins! We are made in God's own image; we are His descendants, His children! For our lifetime, we should live as kings, who have power over unhappiness and negativity in our lives.

I challenge you today to get a bigger vision for your life! See yourself as God sees you! His blessings are infinite! He has crowned you as royalty! Receive that in your spirit, and begin to see positive changes manifest themselves in your life.

Rooted in Christ

I love to plant flowers, making beautiful borders and potted arrangements. During a recent trip to the nursery, I learned something new: pruning. Plants grow fast throughout the year in Texas. They need to be cut way back, so they can go through a new growing cycle. I was told that cutting off all the pretty blooms can actually make the plants thicker, fuller, and able to produce many more blossoms.

Do you ever feel like God is pruning your life? Like He has just about lopped off all you can take? Do not be discouraged. God is just stripping away all the things that are blocking blessings in your life and stifling your faith.

He is our master gardener, and He knows what is best in every area of our lives. We, like plants, need to be shaped, watered, and fed. By pruning, God prepares us for a new life: new blooms, and the beautiful fruit we will eventually produce.

John 15:2 states:

> "HE CUTS OFF EVERY BRANCH OF MINE THAT DOESN'T PRODUCE FRUIT, AND HE PRUNES THE BRANCHES THAT DO BEAR FRUIT SO THEY WILL PRODUCE EVEN MORE."

The more deeply rooted we are in Christ, the more beautiful our harvest will be. The fruit we will produce is the fruit of the spirit.

Galatians 5:22-23 states:

"BUT THE HOLY SPIRIT PRODUCES THIS KIND OF FRUIT IN OUR LIVES: LOVE, JOY, PEACE, PATIENCE, KINDNESS, GOODNESS, FAITHFULNESS, GENTLENESS, AND SELF-CONTROL. THERE IS NO LAW AGAINST THESE THINGS!"

Heavenly Father, we give our lives to You, to prune away all things that keep us from being our best. We know that when You have stripped away all that is not of You, we will be a beautiful new creation, full of joy and happiness.

Living in Excellence

Ecclesiastes 9:10 tells us:

> "WHATEVER YOU DO, DO WELL. FOR WHEN YOU
> GO TO THE GRAVE, THERE WILL BE NO WORK OR
> PLANNING OR KNOWLEDGE OR WISDOM."

When my kids were little, I used to talk to them often about their grades and school work. I expected them to try hard and give it their all. I have always believed that, if you give things your best efforts, then amazing things will happen as a result of your hard work, dedication, and excellence.

It's the classic law of reciprocity. We reap what we sow! Stop doing just enough to get by, unless just getting by is how you want the rest of your life to go. We can always do more. We can always better ourselves. There is always room for improvement. Set better goals and reach for the stars! Get perfect vision for yourself.

Colossians 3:23-24 states:

> "WORK WILLINGLY AT WHATEVER YOU DO,
> AS THOUGH YOU WERE WORKING FOR THE LORD
> RATHER THAN FOR PEOPLE. REMEMBER THAT
> THE LORD WILL GIVE YOU AN INHERITANCE AS
> YOUR REWARD, AND THAT THE MASTER YOU
> ARE SERVING IS CHRIST."

No matter what we do, we should always work as if God is our boss. He is the one who gives us our blessings and abilities. If we work hard, and with integrity, we will be blessed. God can see to it that we get what we deserve. God is always there to do the things that we can't.

Heavenly Father, we want to live a life of excellence that will make You proud. Please, help us with ability, wisdom, and discernment, so we can make wise choices and always try harder. We know you can give us the grace we need to be our best selves and to live our best lives.

Patience

DAY 36

Isaiah 40:31 states:

"BUT THOSE WHO TRUST IN THE LORD WILL FIND NEW STRENGTH. THEY WILL SOAR HIGH ON WINGS LIKE EAGLES. THEY WILL RUN AND NOT GROW WEARY. THEY WILL WALK AND NOT FAINT."

I love to cook. I am boastfully 100% Italian, so I love to make all sorts of wonderful homemade pasta and sauces. I often cooked with my extraordinary grandma when I was a kid. Nothing from a box or can would do for her! She took her time, and patiently and lovingly created fabulous Italian meals from scratch, every single day. I make her meals for very special occasions. For every-day meals, I want dinner on the table quickly, and the resulting mess to be cleaned up even quicker. I lack the patience required to create a feast on a daily basis.

Why don't more people cook from scratch? What has changed over the years? We have become a society of instant gratification. We do everything lightning fast, and grumble over waiting even for the shortest period of time.

Proverbs 14:29 tells us:

"PEOPLE WITH UNDERSTANDING CONTROL THEIR ANGER; A HOT TEMPER SHOWS GREAT FOOLISHNESS."

We lack patience in our everyday lives, and we have an even harder time waiting on God and His perfect timing when we want answers to our prayers. We get frustrated and discouraged because we feel that God is taking way too long.

But, God is always faithful, and will always answer our prayers with His impeccably perfect timing. Wait on Him patiently, and stay positive and joyful! You may be very close to seeing your prayers answered. God may not always be early, but He is never late.

A Page From God's Playbook

Raising boys, I've heard a lot of talk about football over the years! I think about football players and all the hard work they put in during a season. The coach must write hundreds of plays that make up the team's official playbook. Each athlete must memorize, learn, and skillfully execute the plays in this manual.

The playbook is a blueprint. When followed correctly, it is a pathway to a victory. On its own, it is basically worthless. If it just sat on a shelf, if the team didn't use the wisdom in its pages, what good would it be? Used for its intended purpose, however, the information in that book is priceless.

What about our playbook: the Word of the Lord? The Holy Bible is, after all, a brilliant manual, designed to give us all the insight we need to be our best selves. Like the team playbook, what good is it if we keep it in a drawer somewhere? There is knowledge, powerful understanding, and wisdom for us to soak up and abide by on every glorious page.

Jeremiah 29:11 states:

> "FOR I KNOW THE PLANS I HAVE FOR YOU," SAYS THE LORD. "THEY ARE PLANS FOR GOOD AND NOT FOR DISASTER, TO GIVE YOU A FUTURE AND A HOPE."

When God designed our plans, He sat down and wrote them in their entirety. He wrote the whole book, from start to finish.

Psalm 32:8 states:

"THE LORD SAYS, "I WILL GUIDE YOU ALONG
THE BEST PATHWAY FOR YOUR LIFE.
I WILL ADVISE YOU AND WATCH OVER YOU."

God, very similarly to an NFL coach, wrote a playbook for each and every one of us! Every plot, twist, and turn on the pages of our playbook is there for a reason. If we trust Him, God will lead us to victories that we cannot even conceive!

The Narrow Way

Matthew 7:13-14 tells us:

> "YOU CAN ENTER GOD'S KINGDOM ONLY THROUGH
> THE NARROW GATE. THE HIGHWAY TO HELL IS
> BROAD, AND ITS GATE IS WIDE FOR THE MANY WHO
> CHOOSE THAT WAY. BUT THE GATEWAY TO LIFE IS VERY
> NARROW AND THE ROAD IS DIFFICULT,
> AND ONLY A FEW EVER FIND IT."

Being naturally artistic, I am very visual, and my imagination can get the best of me. I decided it would be beneficial to use it to visualize the way I believe God would have my path look.

Proverbs 3:6 states:

> "SEEK HIS WILL IN ALL YOU DO, AND
> HE WILL SHOW YOU WHICH PATH TO TAKE."

I see it as a long, and very beautiful, winding, narrow roadway. I can see back to where I have already traveled, but it's misty up ahead.

Psalm 91:11 states:

> "FOR HE WILL ORDER HIS ANGELS TO
> PROTECT YOU WHEREVER YOU GO."

Legions of heavenly winged angels, dressed in robes of pristine white, line my pathway, directing me and guiding me, illuminating it with their brilliance. They point the way, and watch to see that I will not veer off of my path or stumble. I can look to either side and see unbelievable beauty everywhere. How could I have missed this unparalleled beauty before?

Hebrews 11:1 tells us:

"FAITH SHOWS THE REALITY OF WHAT WE HOPE FOR;
IT IS THE EVIDENCE OF THINGS WE CANNOT SEE."

I need not worry about what lies ahead. God has gone before me. He makes our crooked paths straight.

Thank You, Father, for the perfect path You have chosen for each of us. Give us the strength, ability, and patience we need to follow You on this narrow path of goodness.

Trusting God's Word

The anointed word of the Bible is a miraculous tool for living a life of unmerited favor. The Bible tells us that, when we pray, our prayers WILL NOT return to us void! They simply cannot go unnoticed or be overlooked by God.

Here are a few of my favorites, which I declare for myself and my family on a daily basis. I speak Psalm 91 over my family, and visualize the words covering everyone I love. It begins (Psalm 91:1-2):

> "THOSE WHO LIVE IN THE SHELTER OF THE MOST HIGH WILL FIND REST IN THE SHADOW OF THE ALMIGHTY. THIS I DECLARE ABOUT THE LORD: HE ALONE IS MY REFUGE, MY PLACE OF SAFETY; HE IS MY GOD, AND I TRUST HIM."

Line by line, it goes on to tell of the blessings and protection God gives us. He will cover us under His wings, and He will be a shield for us. He has given us our very own army of angels to guard us. And, what do we have to do to merit this? We only need to call on Him!

Another favorite is Ephesians 3:20:

> "NOW ALL GLORY TO GOD, WHO IS ABLE, THROUGH HIS MIGHTY POWER AT WORK WITHIN US, TO ACCOMPLISH INFINITELY MORE THAN WE MIGHT ASK OR THINK."

That is simply amazing to ponder. The blessings will find us! We do not have to go in search of them; we just need to give our hearts to Christ and let Him do the rest.

2 Samuel 22:31 states:

"GOD'S WAY IS PERFECT. ALL THE LORD'S PROMISES PROVE TRUE. HE IS A SHIELD FOR ALL WHO LOOK TO HIM FOR PROTECTION."

Do not let another minute go by without claiming your inheritance through these and all scriptures! Boldly pronounce them over yourself and your loved ones.

Dear Lord, thank You for loving us so much, and for giving us all of these wonderful promises in Your Word!

The God Habit   DAY 40

Are you a creature of habit? Good habits can be quite beneficial. Why not get in the one habit that can change your life forever, in amazing ways? Get in the "God habit!"

Matthew 6:33 states:

> "SEEK THE KINGDOM OF GOD ABOVE ALL ELSE, AND LIVE RIGHTEOUSLY, AND HE WILL GIVE YOU EVERYTHING YOU NEED."

This verse tells us not to just seek God, but to seek Him first! Give Him the best part of us, the first part of our days.

I am very much a routine kind of person. My morning time spent with God is very important to me. I grab my Bible, my scripture-filled journal, and my cozy throw, and nestle into my favorite place on the sunroom sofa. There, I wholeheartedly bask in the presence of my precious Lord and Savior.

My "God habit" is like essential food for my soul: it jump-starts my day, and fills me with abundant expectation. The word of God replenishes my faith and restores my joy. I can leave all my cares with Him and go about enjoying my day, knowing that God is looking out for me.

Proverbs 4:20-21 tells us:

> "MY CHILD, PAY ATTENTION TO WHAT I SAY. LISTEN CAREFULLY TO MY WORDS. DON'T LOSE SIGHT OF THEM. LET THEM PENETRATE DEEP INTO YOUR HEART."

On days when my routine is interrupted, everything feels wrong . It feels like I have to do everything the hard way. I realize that my "God habit" keeps me closely tethered to Him. When we do not stay focused on Him, our paths get blurry, and much wider, leaving more room for us to stray and make bad choices. The more days that go by without spending time with God, the harder it becomes to let Him in.

I challenge you to get in the "God habit!" I promise, the more time you spend with Him, the more faith-filled and richly blessed your life will be. Do not waste another day!

Guard Your Thoughts

Our thoughts are powerful mind-invaders that can make us or break us. They can lead to a blessed, faith-filled life, or keep us locked up in the bondage of mediocrity, lack, and infirmity.

2 Corinthians 10:5 states:

> "WE DESTROY EVERY PROUD OBSTACLE
> THAT KEEPS PEOPLE FROM KNOWING GOD.
> WE CAPTURE THEIR REBELLIOUS THOUGHTS
> AND TEACH THEM TO OBEY CHRIST."

Our thoughts must be held captive, so that they cannot overtake our lives and handcuff our future. The Bible says our thoughts are not our own! Good, warm, loving thoughts are from the Lord, while negative, anxious, and evil thoughts come straight from the enemy himself. The good news is that we get to choose what we spend our time thinking about.

Romans 12:2 tells us:

> "DON'T COPY THE BEHAVIOR AND CUSTOMS OF THIS
> WORLD, BUT LET GOD TRANSFORM YOU INTO A NEW
> PERSON BY CHANGING THE WAY YOU THINK. THEN
> YOU WILL LEARN TO KNOW GOD'S WILL FOR YOU,
> WHICH IS GOOD AND PLEASING AND PERFECT."

The Bible says we should cast down all thoughts that come against the perfect will of God. "To cast" means to throw with force, to hurl!

Proverbs 23:7 states:

"FOR AS HE THINKETH IN HIS HEART, SO IS HE."

Positive or negative, what we think is what we become!

The Bible lists the things we should spend our time focusing on in Philippians 4:8:

"AND NOW, DEAR BROTHERS AND SISTERS, ONE FINAL THING. FIX YOUR THOUGHTS ON WHAT IS TRUE, AND HONORABLE, AND RIGHT, AND PURE, AND LOVELY, AND ADMIRABLE. THINK ABOUT THINGS THAT ARE EXCELLENT AND WORTHY OF PRAISE."

Get in the habit of perpetual positive thinking! Get into the word of God! Thank You, sweet Father in Heaven, for helping us guard our thoughts and stay focused on You. Please, continue to help us think God-like thoughts!

God Is the Great I AM

Exodus 3:14-15 states:

"GOD REPLIED TO MOSES, "I AM WHO I AM. SAY THIS TO THE PEOPLE OF ISRAEL: I AM HAS SENT ME TO YOU."

Two small words, three simple letters: "I AM." The Lord tells us repeatedly, in His Word, that He is the great "I AM." I've thought about that, and wondered why He never added anything else to that statement. I felt like He was leaving out all the awe-inspiring adjectives that He could have used to enhance His own resume. Yet, He chose not to. These two powerful and simple words say more about God than an entire library ever could.

HE JUST IS!

Those words are meant to be followed by whatever we need God to be at the time. We get to fill in the blanks! There's no limit on how many ways He can fill in those voids. In other words, what do you need God to be today?

Isaiah 9:6 states:

"FOR A CHILD IS BORN TO US, A SON IS GIVEN TO US. THE GOVERNMENT WILL REST ON HIS SHOULDERS. AND HE WILL BE CALLED: WONDERFUL COUNSELOR, MIGHTY GOD, EVERLASTING FATHER, PRINCE OF PEACE."

When we are lonesome, God is our loving companion. He is our bountiful source when we fall on hard times. He is our divine healer when we are sick. He is our powerful protector who keeps us safe from harm. He is the teacher who fills us with knowledge. He is the architect who draws the blueprints of our lives. He anoints us with talents, abilities, and purpose.

John 8:58 tells us:

"JESUS ANSWERED, "I TELL YOU THE TRUTH,
BEFORE ABRAHAM WAS EVEN BORN, I AM!"

Whatever you need today, boldly go to the throne and call on God. He is there, ready and willing, wearing one of His many hats! God is all you will ever need. He is the great "I AM!"

The Big Picture

Hebrews 11:1 states:

"FAITH SHOWS THE REALITY OF WHAT WE HOPE FOR;
IT IS THE EVIDENCE OF THINGS WE CANNOT SEE."

Have you ever tried to put together one of those giant jigsaw puzzles that has at least a thousand pieces? When you first open the box, it's hard to imagine that each little piece is significant to the full picture. But, when you put them all together, a wonderful picture starts to emerge: the bigger picture. Sound familiar?

Isaiah 46:10:

"ONLY I CAN TELL YOU THE FUTURE BEFORE IT
EVEN HAPPENS. EVERYTHING I PLAN WILL COME
TO PASS, FOR I DO WHATEVER I WISH."

God is the creator of the great puzzle called life. Each one of us has our own unique puzzle box with an amazing picture on it. We cannot ever see this picture; only God Himself knows what our finished puzzle will look like.

When we are going through a hard time, we need only to remember that this is just one tiny piece of our puzzle. If this piece were missing, the puzzle would be incomplete.

Why don't we get to see more than a tiny piece of the puzzle at a time? God designed us that way, so we must put our focus and trust in Him. Uncertainty builds faith in our wonderfully omniscient, all-powerful God.

Enjoy your life, day by day, piece by piece. Do not worry about tomorrow today — let God be God! He is already holding the next puzzle piece with the answer you have been praying for. Remember that God is completely in control, and He always sees the bigger picture!

Setting Goals

Philippians 3:13-14 states:

"FORGETTING THE PAST AND LOOKING FORWARD TO WHAT LIES AHEAD, I PRESS ON TO REACH THE END OF THE RACE AND RECEIVE THE HEAVENLY PRIZE FOR WHICH GOD, THROUGH CHRIST JESUS, IS CALLING US."

A goal is an end toward which effort is directed. Why do we need goals? Why are they so important to living our best life? Not having a goal is a recipe for maintaining the status quo and mediocrity. Writing down your goals is a small action that can get the ball rolling. So, go grab a piece of paper and a pen. Go ahead, I'll wait...

You should know what's next! Write your most dear, from-the-heart goals! Do not write only what you think you can accomplish right now. In big, bold letters, confidently write what YOU REALLY WANT to do.

Don't sell yourself short. Our dreams and desires come from the Lord! The scripture above clearly states that the things we can accomplish are an upward calling from God. We are meant to rise higher; we are to live out our divine purpose, and fulfill our God-given destiny.

Why would God ever give us a dream that we were incapable of obtaining? Why would He give us talents to be wasted and not used? Luke 1:37 states:

"FOR NOTHING IS IMPOSSIBLE WITH GOD."

That's right! Visualize yourself having already accomplished your goals. See every last detail, and spend time each day nurturing that vision. If you have a goal and a dream, do not let anyone — including yourself — tell you all the reasons why it won't happen. Tell yourself all the reasons why it will!

Heavenly Father, You gave us our dreams, talents, and desires. Help us stay focused and trust You to help us see them come to pass!

God Will Never Leave You

1 Peter 5:7 states:

> "GIVE ALL YOUR WORRIES AND CARES TO GOD,
> FOR HE CARES ABOUT YOU."

How many of you remember those old commercials about the Maytag appliance repair man? They showed a sweet, older gentleman in a Maytag uniform, waiting in a lonely office for the phone to ring. The idea was that the appliances were so well-made that his services were never needed. You could not help but love the sweet Maytag repairman, but you also felt very sad for him. He was a man without a purpose.

I sometimes picture God that way. I think we often neglect Him and try to go it alone. We forget that He is always right there, waiting to help us, and all we have to do is ask.

Why does it seem that we only turn to Him in a crisis, or when we are in panic mode? Some people have this misconception that God should not be bothered with all the little, mundane occurrences in our lives. They think that He has much bigger issues and "real" problems to solve. This could not be further from the truth! He wants to be part of our everyday lives.

Proverbs 3:6 states:

> "SEEK HIS WILL IN ALL YOU DO, AND HE
> WILL SHOW YOU WHICH PATH TO TAKE."

All means ALL! Not some, and not just what you deem important enough to let God be in charge of. We mustn't leave God sitting all alone, waiting for our phone call. Let Him lead you. He is the universe's greatest repairman. And, unlike Maytag appliances, we constantly need repairs. We will never not need God!

Thank You, Father, that You are always with me, holding my hand through life, and carrying me when I'm too tired to do it alone. I only need to call Your name.

Giving It All to God

James 1:2-4 states:

> "DEAR BROTHERS AND SISTERS, WHEN TROUBLES OF ANY KIND COME YOUR WAY, CONSIDER IT AN OPPORTUNITY FOR GREAT JOY. FOR YOU KNOW THAT WHEN YOUR FAITH IS TESTED, YOUR ENDURANCE HAS A CHANCE TO GROW. SO LET IT GROW, FOR WHEN YOUR ENDURANCE IS FULLY DEVELOPED, YOU WILL BE PERFECT AND COMPLETE, NEEDING NOTHING."

Sometimes, we go through some tough times in our lives. We agonize over our fears and let them take over. We become so entrenched in our problems that we fail to see what God does for us every day.

The enemy loves distracting us and making us fear things. When we are focused on our problems, we lose focus on God. Before we know it, fear, like an old record playing in the background of our mind, becomes part of us. But, God is in control.

Romans 12:2 states:

> "DON'T COPY THE BEHAVIOR AND CUSTOMS OF THIS WORLD, BUT LET GOD TRANSFORM YOU INTO A NEW PERSON BY CHANGING THE WAY YOU THINK. THEN YOU WILL LEARN TO KNOW GOD'S WILL FOR YOU, WHICH IS GOOD AND PLEASING AND PERFECT."

Renewing our minds — doesn't that sound brilliant?

We often fail in our own attempts because we are operating in the flesh. We are settling for a life that is deeply rooted in pain, instead of letting God take over. The good news is that our old insecurities can be transformed and replaced with pure joy! We must let go of fear and let God in!

Heavenly Father, I cry out to You now. I know You hear my prayers and You love me. I need You to show me that. I need a miracle. You know where I am right now, and I thank you for loving me perfectly.

God Will Fight For You

Psalm 34:19 states:

> "THE RIGHTEOUS PERSON FACES MANY TROUBLES,
> BUT THE LORD COMES TO THE RESCUE EACH TIME."

We often stand in the midst of a storm, clinging and hanging on as we look out onto a sea of adversities. The storms of chaos and turmoil threaten us and make us doubt what we already know. We grieve, we fret, we cry — but, if we are to look up, we can see through it all. We can see straight to the amazing love and unending grace of our loving Father. He's there, unwavering in His strength and protection. His whispers speak to our deepest soul and inner thoughts. He lovingly encourages us with His strong voice.

Isaiah 43:2 states:

> "WHEN YOU GO THROUGH DEEP WATERS,
> I WILL BE WITH YOU. WHEN YOU GO THROUGH
> RIVERS OF DIFFICULTY, YOU WILL NOT DROWN.
> WHEN YOU WALK THROUGH THE FIRE OF OPPRESSION,
> YOU WILL NOT BE BURNED UP; THE FLAMES WILL
> NOT CONSUME YOU."

God will not let you stumble and fall. He sees all, and He fights for you! He battles it all on your behalf.

Stay calm in the storm, because your rescuer is coming. When you trust Him, regardless of what tries to pry you loose from His grasp, He will hold you even tighter.

Thank You, sweet Father, that You are right here with us, carrying us through our trials. We praise You in advance for our victories! No weapon formed against us will ever prosper!

Walk in the Light

It seems like we are constantly seeking something. Oftentimes, we can't even put our finger on what it is. What's missing? Why do we often feel so lonely, even when we're in a room full of people? Why do we buy things we don't need, or eat when we are not hungry?

Psalm 63:1 states:

> "O GOD, YOU ARE MY GOD; I EARNESTLY SEARCH
> FOR YOU. MY SOUL THIRSTS FOR YOU; MY WHOLE
> BODY LONGS FOR YOU IN THIS PARCHED AND
> WEARY LAND WHERE THERE IS NO WATER."

God is what's missing! He is the one and only way to achieve pure, sweet, peaceful contentment. If you do not have that divine closeness to your Creator, you can never feel completely fulfilled. You will be constantly seeking something that is missing and never finding it.

Job 33:28 states:

> "GOD RESCUED ME FROM THE GRAVE,
> AND NOW MY LIFE IS FILLED WITH LIGHT."

When we follow our desires for instant gratification, we wind up in a lowly pit of calamity and destruction. How many marriages are destroyed by adultery? How many people have substantial credit card debt because impulse buying gave them a moment of euphoria? These are just a couple of the countless other examples of people walking aimlessly down the path of destruction. The peace they search for can ONLY be found in the presence of Jesus!

1 John 1:7 states:

> "BUT, IF WE ARE LIVING IN THE LIGHT, AS GOD
> IS IN THE LIGHT, THEN WE HAVE FELLOWSHIP
> WITH EACH OTHER, AND THE BLOOD OF JESUS,
> HIS SON, CLEANSES US FROM ALL SIN."

We begin to see that all of our needs are being met when we focus on God.

Heavenly Father, we long to follow Your path, and bask in Your light as You remove the darkness from us. Thank you for filling us with Your grace and mercy as we draw closer to You today.

We Are God's Heirs

Did you know you are an heir to a royal throne? You have a mighty inheritance that was promised to you. Your ancestry can be traced to the King of all Kings! We are the sons and daughters of God Himself.

It's amazing to realize that we are the heirs of the creator of the universe. We did not have to do anything to deserve all the riches and blessings He has in store for us. He is our loving Father —a daddy like any other, who loves to bless His children!

Romans 8:17 states:

"AND SINCE WE ARE HIS CHILDREN, WE ARE HIS HEIRS. IN FACT, TOGETHER WITH CHRIST WE ARE HEIRS OF GOD'S GLORY. BUT IF WE ARE TO SHARE HIS GLORY, WE MUST ALSO SHARE HIS SUFFERING."

My own two sons are adults now. When they were growing up, they were so comfortable knowing that what was mine was also theirs. They did not have to worry about anything. They never felt like they had to earn the right to my unconditional love, our home, or anything I provided.

If we, as parents, want to bless our children, how much more does our loving Creator, the one who designed and intricately planned out every detail of our lives, want to bless us?

We pray for God's will to be done on Earth as it is in Heaven. This means that all of the wonderful things of Heaven are what God, our Father, wants for us all to have and enjoy here on Earth today!

Heavenly Father, thank You for loving us so much that You have made us heirs to Your Kingdom of Heaven. Thank You for the blessings You pour on us, Your beloved children.

Getting Your Joy Back

Does it ever seem to you like you just woke up one day and your joy was gone? Did it happen all of a sudden, or was it gradual?

John 10:10 states:

> "THE THIEF COMES ONLY TO STEAL AND KILL AND DESTROY; I HAVE COME THAT THEY MAY HAVE LIFE, AND HAVE IT TO THE FULL."

The enemy is that despised thief in the night, that robs and steals joy from us. He tries to take everything good that Jesus suffered and died for us to have.

But, did you know you have complete authority over the enemy? Through the blood of Jesus at His crucifixion, we have power that defeats all of Satan's plans. No matter what the enemy tries to do to us, we will always win! When we feel ourselves getting down, depressed, or fearful, we must be armed for battle; we must know the Word in order to be equipped with the best defense! Say the name of Jesus, and the enemy flees!

So, how do we get back those things the enemy steals from us? How do we restore and maintain our joy?

The good news is that God is also in the restoration business! God says, where there is pain in the night, joy comes in the morning. When you are feeling down, get in the presence of God.

Psalm 16:11 tells us:

"YOU WILL SHOW ME THE WAY OF LIFE,
GRANTING ME THE JOY OF YOUR PRESENCE AND
THE PLEASURES OF LIVING WITH YOU FOREVER."

Heavenly Father, I praise You today for restoring joy unto me.

Being Bold for God

I was seated in a lobby, waiting on an oil change for my car. I noticed that each person in the room was using smartphones or tablets, oblivious to their surroundings. What has happened to good, old-fashioned, friendly conversation?

As Christians, we are called to be an example in this world. We are called to break through the barriers of computer screens and offer a real human voice. We are to be bold for the Lord and become His mouthpiece on Earth.

Acts 28:31 says we should be:

"BOLDLY PROCLAIMING THE KINGDOM OF GOD
AND TEACHING ABOUT THE LORD JESUS CHRIST..."

We may be the only chance that person seated near us will ever get to hear about how much God loves them. We should never miss an opportunity to spread the good news of Jesus!

Mark 16:15 states:

"AND THEN HE TOLD THEM, "GO INTO ALL
THE WORLD AND PREACH THE GOOD NEWS
TO EVERYONE."

The Good News should be shared with the entire world! As Christians, we often think that this refers to the missionaries spreading The Gospel in remote parts of the Earth. But, the man seated next to you in a lobby on a Wednesday afternoon is every bit as important to God. It's no accident that you are near a certain person on a particular day. We all have divine appointments, set up in advance by God.

I challenge you to live in boldness for God. Before leaving your house, ask Him to put someone in your path today that needs to hear an encouraging word of hope.

Thank You, Father, for the boldness to be a light to those in need. Let us not be afraid to be a witness for You today. Give us people today that need our encouragement. Let Your words be our words!

God Will Provide

Being from a large Italian family, some of my most cherished memories involve my grandmother lovingly making food from scratch. My grandmother was always prepared. To her, it was a crime to not have a freezer full of "just in case" lasagna and cannoli, should she entertain company.

I've thought about the children of Israel, wandering in the wilderness. They needed to rely on God to provide manna each day. They were not allowed to take any more than a single day's portion — if they did, it would immediately rot. There would be no "just in case" food. Can you imagine the vulnerability of being a parent of young children, and having no stocked pantry or extra food at all?

God wants us to trust Him. He asks us to tell Him what we need.

By commanding that the Israelites not collect any more food than they needed for one day, God was asking them to take a leap of faith, and to rely on His merciful grace.

Sometimes, our trials seem overwhelming and impossible to manage. But, then God shows up, with a daily helping of His amazing grace, a fresh batch of heavenly manna. He says, "Trust me! We will get through this together today. I will be here again tomorrow, and we will handle tomorrow then."

Matthew 6:25-26 states:

"THAT IS WHY I TELL YOU NOT TO WORRY ABOUT EVERYDAY LIFE—WHETHER YOU HAVE ENOUGH FOOD AND DRINK, OR ENOUGH CLOTHES TO WEAR. ISN'T LIFE MORE THAN FOOD, AND YOUR BODY MORE

THAN CLOTHING? LOOK AT THE BIRDS. THEY DON'T PLANT OR HARVEST OR STORE FOOD IN BARNS, FOR YOUR HEAVENLY FATHER FEEDS THEM. AND AREN'T YOU FAR MORE VALUABLE TO HIM THAN THEY ARE?"

Heavenly Father, thank You for providing for us all. You give us food for our bodies and grace for our souls every day!

But God...

Genesis 50:20 states:

"YOU INTENDED TO HARM ME, BUT GOD INTENDED IT ALL FOR GOOD. HE BROUGHT ME TO THIS POSITION SO I COULD SAVE THE LIVES OF MANY PEOPLE."

Sadly, in our lives, we all go through gut-wrenching trials. But, when tribulation takes us to our knees, it beckons us to go so much deeper into our faith. Without the turmoil, we would never know the sheer enormity of the Lord's pure love. Is this not the very reason for a trial?

Pain, lies, and betrayal can level our lives, and can change our worlds in an instant. Life can certainly throw you a curve ball and make you want to shout, "I quit! I'm done. I GIVE UP!"

Well, there's a "but" — BUT GOD.

In our sorrows of the flesh we utter:

But God, where are you?

But God, it hurts so much.

But God, if you love me, then why do I have to suffer like this?

However, we need to remember that faith is what we cannot see! We must change these statements to reflect our faith:

But God is always here!

But God knows your suffering and your pain, and wants to comfort you!

But God will never leave you or forsake you!

But God will turn all things around for your good!

But God's plan is more than we could ever ask or imagine!

Psalm 34:18 states:

"THE LORD IS CLOSE TO THE BROKENHEARTED;
HE RESCUES THOSE WHOSE SPIRITS ARE CRUSHED."

God's got you covered. You're going to get your breakthrough! That is a promise. It's not going to be without pain or effort, BUT GOD will demonstrate His love and mercy in the midst of your worst circumstances. It will get better. The answer is on the way!

Getting Connected to God

Matthew 19:26 states:

> "JESUS LOOKED AT THEM INTENTLY AND SAID,
> 'HUMANLY SPEAKING, IT IS IMPOSSIBLE. BUT WITH
> GOD EVERYTHING IS POSSIBLE.'"

Without our smartphones and tablets, we'd be lost! Without technology, we would feel as though we had no links to the outside world. These electronic gadgets are the only way we have a clue what day and time we are to be where. Our cell phones and computers require plugging into a power source and charging, so that they can serve their purpose. We need cell towers, data plans, Internet providers, and secure passwords to stay linked to everyone and everything all the time. Have you ever thought about how much trust and reliance we place in these devices to run our lives?

John 15:5 states:

> "YES, I AM THE VINE; YOU ARE THE BRANCHES.
> THOSE WHO REMAIN IN ME, AND I IN THEM,
> WILL PRODUCE MUCH FRUIT. FOR APART FROM
> ME YOU CAN DO NOTHING."

This Bible verse proves that we must stay connected to God, our constant source! Branches cannot live if they are cut off from a tree or a vine.

What if we placed trust in our Lord every day, to help us handle everything that the day will bring? What if we stay plugged into the ultimate power source? God's connection is always reliable, and it can't interrupt or break.

God is the power source! What purpose are we serving if we aren't fully charged and plugged into our power source every day?

Stay fully connected to the divine love and wisdom of your Heavenly Father, the one who created you, by wholeheartedly trusting in Him. By praying, reading the word, and following His divine purpose for your life, you can stay connected to Him all the time.

Beauty for Ashes

Job 42:12 states:

> "SO THE LORD BLESSED JOB IN THE SECOND HALF
> OF HIS LIFE EVEN MORE THAN IN THE BEGINNING.
> FOR NOW HE HAD 14,000 SHEEP, 6,000 CAMELS, 1,000
> TEAMS OF OXEN, AND 1,000 FEMALE DONKEYS."

I remember the most difficult year I have ever faced. At the end of it, I found myself in an airport, taking an international flight. Coincidentally, I just so happened to be flying on my birthday. It felt like I was jetting off to a latter part of my life, leaving what lay behind and looking forward to all the future blessings that God had been stockpiling for me.

Romans 8:28 states:

> "AND WE KNOW THAT GOD CAUSES EVERYTHING
> TO WORK TOGETHER FOR THE GOOD OF THOSE
> WHO LOVE GOD AND ARE CALLED ACCORDING
> TO HIS PURPOSE FOR THEM."

After a 10+ hour flight, I arrived in Scotland, a place of unmatched beauty. It was time to breathe! My travels on that trip also took me to London, the English countryside, and to Paris. God's peace was in every laugh, every train ride, and every glorious croissant or café au lait that I ate or drank. This was beauty for ashes: a double portion of all that the enemy had tried to steal from me.

I am reminded that we sometimes must go through the tough times in life to get to the good days. God has to prune things away from our lives that rob us of what He has in store for us; He has to take away the joy-stealers that leach onto us and keep us from His best. He really does turn ALL things around for the good!

God is who He says He is. When you're in darkness, hold on! Your best days are still out in front of you!

Wanting It All

I sometimes wonder: What is behind the crazy mindset of perpetually wanting what we can't have? Why is it that we can never be fully satisfied right where we are? There is an anxiousness and a restlessness that keeps us in a constant inner struggle, in search of the next best thing. Our incessant yearning creates an insatiable pit in us that, by the world's standards, can never truly be filled.

Mark 8:36 asks:

> "AND WHAT DO YOU BENEFIT IF YOU GAIN THE
> WHOLE WORLD BUT LOSE YOUR OWN SOUL?"

We seem to be missing the whole point of having a blessed life: We should be enjoying it now! We should be resting in a divine peace, right where we are, not caught up in an exhausting search to have it all.

Psalm 118:24 declares:

> "THIS IS THE DAY THE LORD HAS MADE.
> WE WILL REJOICE AND BE GLAD IN IT."

God wants us to enjoy every moment and to live in the present! Don't worry about tomorrow today. There are always going to be things to strive for, and we should always want to better ourselves and look forward to a glorious future in Christ. But, that all comes with first being grateful for and enjoying all that God has set before us today!

Matthew 6:33 tells us:

"SEEK THE KINGDOM OF GOD ABOVE ALL ELSE,
AND LIVE RIGHTEOUSLY, AND HE WILL GIVE
YOU EVERYTHING YOU NEED."

Don't ignore small beginnings. When you appreciate all that you have and where you are, and you enjoy this very moment in time — that's when God can truly bless you with more of His brilliant and unending glory. We must be truly thankful for the here and now!

God Does Not Change

Hebrews 13:8 states:

"JESUS IS THE SAME YESTERDAY, TODAY, AND FOREVER."

A recent get-together with some childhood friends sparked nostalgia for the "good old days." Remember when days were carefree, and summer seemed endless? My friends and I practically lived outside; the first glimmer of the street lamps was the only cue to return home. We drank out of the hose, caught fireflies in jars, and rode on the handlebars of our bikes.

Our hang out was the local drive-in, where everyone showed up at dusk for ice cream and root-beer floats. In my memory, the few square miles of our tiny Illinois town seemed larger than life. It was a patch of wholesomeness, carved from the midst of a cornfield canvas. We felt safe; we knew everyone in town. No one locked their doors because there was no need.

The "good old days" are gone. These days, it seems we are living and breathing change at breakneck speed. It seems nothing is guaranteed anymore, other than change. It's coming, whether you're ready or not.

Psalm 119:89 tells us:

"YOUR ETERNAL WORD, O LORD,
STANDS FIRM IN HEAVEN."

In our earthly lives, virtually nothing stays the same. There is one thing, though, that remains constant: our infallible Creator!

He reigns supreme for all eternity. We can count on that! No matter what changes, and no matter how much insecurity that causes us, God is never going to change!

Ecclesiastes 3:14 states:

"AND I KNOW THAT WHATEVER GOD DOES IS FINAL. NOTHING CAN BE ADDED TO IT OR TAKEN FROM IT. GOD'S PURPOSE IS THAT PEOPLE SHOULD FEAR HIM."

Spend time reading the Word, and being in the presence of God. As you seek a lasting and close relationship with our Father, you will see His character, and you will see that the more things change, the more God stays the same.

Getting a New Vision

Proverbs 29:18 states:

> "WHERE THERE IS NO VISION, THE PEOPLE PERISH:
> BUT HE THAT KEEPETH THE LAW, HAPPY IS HE."

I am sure that, at one point or another, we all get stuck in a rut, or we get a little sick and tired of what we are doing in our lives. So, does a case of the doldrums mean we're not doing the right thing? Have we messed up and missed our calling?

No. On the contrary, I believe that a little restlessness now and then is good for us. Being uncomfortable helps motivate us and push us further. Feeling unsettled causes us to think about how we can better use our time, efforts, and talent to further glorify God through our own gifts and callings.

When we have a vision, we can see our victory. There is a shift in our mindset; we have a fresh new zest for life, and a zeal to live deliberately. A new vision can jump start action and create plans.

It is not God's will for us to remain stalled and without motivation to succeed. His master plan is to propel us forward, from great achievement to greater achievement.

Acts 2:17 tells us:

> "'IN THE LAST DAYS,' GOD SAYS, 'I WILL POUR
> OUT MY SPIRIT UPON ALL PEOPLE. YOUR SONS
> AND DAUGHTERS WILL PROPHESY. YOUR YOUNG
> MEN WILL SEE VISIONS, AND YOUR OLD MEN
> WILL DREAM DREAMS.'"

This scripture tells us that God is the one who gives us the visions. He allows uneasiness in our lives so we can turn to Him and receive a fresh outpouring of support from the master visionary.

What visions do you have for yourself? What is God putting in your heart that you have been putting off? Put on your rose-colored glasses and see it. Then, go get it! God doesn't call the qualified; He qualifies the called!

Beginning Again

Zechariah 4:7 states:

> "NOTHING, NOT EVEN A MIGHTY MOUNTAIN,
> WILL STAND IN ZERUBBABEL'S WAY; IT WILL
> BECOME A LEVEL PLAIN BEFORE HIM! AND WHEN
> ZERUBBABEL SETS THE FINAL STONE OF THE
> TEMPLE IN PLACE, THE PEOPLE WILL SHOUT:
> 'MAY GOD BLESS IT! MAY GOD BLESS IT!'"

Recently, while I was cleaning out my garage, I happened across a 30-gallon storage tub filled with items that were bought for certain projects that I was fully interested in pursuing, but never got around to. It got me wondering what else in my life I may have left unfinished.

I'm sure this happens to many of us, and sometimes, we don't know how we could possibly begin again. But, when God gives you something to do, He always gives you the enabling grace to do it, regardless of how daunting it may seem.

We should never want to be in the same place too long, because we want thirst and hunger for more, to always be growing in our relationship with the Lord.

What is God asking you to resurrect today? What dreams and ideas have you been laying aside? What have you avoided because of the enemy's voice whispering thoughts of failure? The enemy loves nothing more than to see us abandon that which God intended for our blessing.

God will not stop. He hasn't given up on you; His vision for you still stands. Whatever is left unfinished, whatever you have failed to accomplish — God will remind you that it's time to begin again!

Forgiving Once More

I was enjoying a walk on a beautiful warm day when, out of nowhere, a sudden onslaught of bad memories came flooding to my mind. They were related to betrayal I had suffered. I immediately recognized the bullying for what it was: The enemy was bringing up all this old pain and taunting me with it.

I thought, instead, of James 4:7:

> "SUBMIT YOURSELVES, THEN, TO GOD.
> RESIST THE DEVIL, AND HE WILL FLEE FROM YOU."

So, I submitted myself to God. I asked God to, once again, help me forgive those who had betrayed me, and then — and this was even harder — I asked God to bless them.

Don't think for a minute that this was easy. It can be, by far, one of the hardest things God asks us to do.

Matthew 18:21-22 tells us:

> "THEN, PETER CAME TO JESUS AND ASKED,
> 'LORD, HOW MANY TIMES SHALL I FORGIVE MY
> BROTHER OR SISTER WHO SINS AGAINST ME?
> UP TO SEVEN TIMES?'
> JESUS ANSWERED, 'I TELL YOU, NOT SEVEN TIMES,
> BUT SEVENTY TIMES SEVEN.'"

Seventy times seven is a lot of times!. Christ is lovingly telling us in this scripture that He knows forgiveness is hard. We need our loving Father to enable us to keep forgiving those who have wronged us, over and over again.

Forgiveness does NOT excuse the behavior of those who hurt you. Leave it to God to judge them. Forgiveness benefits you; by not forgiving, you continue to hurt yourself. The enemy knows that if he can continually stir up hatred and contempt for those who have hurt you, he will successfully block you from moving forward in the glorious victory that God has in store for you!

Lord, we seek Your strength as we forgive those who have hurt us, in the same manner in which You have so generously forgiven us. We ask for Your peace and joy as You lovingly heal our souls.

Forgetting the Past

Philippians 3:13 states:

> "NO, DEAR BROTHERS AND SISTERS,
> I HAVE NOT ACHIEVED IT, BUT I FOCUS ON
> THIS ONE THING: FORGETTING THE PAST, AND
> LOOKING FORWARD TO WHAT LIES AHEAD."

I believe God wants us to know that many of us are on a continuous vacation from reality. The vacation is actually a staycation, one in which we never really reach the beautiful, serene happiness of eternal joy here on Earth. We are stuck in the stronghold of our own limitations. We are continually checking our past in our rear view mirror, stopping to look back with regret, guilt, and shame.

The trouble with that is that it zaps our energy and inhibits our momentum. We can't move forward. Our propulsion is faulty. We become complacent, numb, and addicted to the cycle of being stuck. We blame our circumstances for our lot in life. We feel stuck on a bridge to nowhere.

Break the cycle, and believe you are a child of God! With that mindset, you will be eternally propelled from great achievement to greater achievement! You will live the purpose that Jesus Christ, our Lord and Savior, has designated for you. Let this be done to you according to His will. Step out in faith. Grab hold of the promises of the Kingdom of Heaven, and receive that which our Savior has so lovingly bestowed upon you! Make sure not to miss it!

Starting today, embrace the present with fresh gusto. Forget the past! Declare that you are constantly blessed and victory will chase you down!

The Desires of the Heart

Psalm 37:4 states:

> "TAKE DELIGHT IN THE LORD, AND HE WILL
> GIVE YOU YOUR HEART'S DESIRES."

What are the desires of your heart? Are they the things you really think you want? The things you secretly desire and hope for? The things you think will bring you continuous joy?

I thought about the meaning of that scripture, and decided that we are looking at our desires the wrong way.

When we draw near to God, He shows us what He wants us to desire. When He gives us the "desires of our hearts," He is not giving us all the things we want, but the desire to want what He wants us to have.

Philippians 2:13 states:

> "FOR GOD IS WORKING IN YOU, GIVING YOU THE
> DESIRE AND THE POWER TO DO WHAT PLEASES HIM."

God wants us to follow Him, love Him, trust Him, and receive Him with our whole hearts. When we have a relationship with God, all of our wants of the flesh become trivial.

Make it your desire to surrender your days to Him. Spend more time seeking Him, and praising and worshiping Him.

Matthew 6:33 states:

"Seek the Kingdom of God above all else, and live righteously, and He will give you everything you need."

Give Him the best part of you first, and He will give you His perfect peace and the desires of your heart.

Believing God

Can you believe that there is a whole tree in just one tiny seed? We plant seeds believing and trusting that eventually a tree would grow out of it and flourish.

All seeds are planted in the darkness of soil, but they eventually make their way to the light, and flourish through sheer determination.

Faith is a process. No matter how you feel, and how difficult things seem — believe God anyway! If you are missing faith, sow a seed of giving, no matter how small. God doesn't look at the amount, He looks at your heart. You can always give of your time and gifts.

Whatever you're going through, when you feel discouraged, plant a seed of victory. Don't remain anchored to your doubts. Speak the truth of God's holy living Word.

Philippians 4:19 states:

"AND THIS SAME GOD WHO TAKES CARE OF ME WILL SUPPLY ALL YOUR NEEDS FROM HIS GLORIOUS RICHES, WHICH HAVE BEEN GIVEN TO US IN CHRIST JESUS."

What do you want God to do for you? Ask Him! Don't ask too small. Who do you think you are talking to when you pray? You are talking to the Creator of the universe. He owns the entire world, and everything in it! Plant huge, kingdom-sized seeds of faith. Believe!

Don't disqualify yourself. See it in your mind; believe it with your heart! Declare victoriously out loud, "I am a candidate for the miraculous." Whether you feel like it or not, never lose faith in God!

Being a Better You

Romans 12:2 tells us:

"DON'T COPY THE BEHAVIOR AND CUSTOMS OF THIS
WORLD, BUT LET GOD TRANSFORM YOU INTO A NEW
PERSON BY CHANGING THE WAY YOU THINK. THEN
YOU WILL LEARN TO KNOW GOD'S WILL FOR YOU,
WHICH IS GOOD AND PLEASING AND PERFECT."

Renew your mind daily though praise and prayer, and become
a better you. Enrich yourself deeply and wisely from God's book.
Learn and perpetually grow in knowledge from the Bible, His holy,
living Word. Meet God daily, as you seek Him first by coming into
a place of thanksgiving for the extent of your blessings. Wholeheartedly soak in the presence of the Lord as you search His word
for guidance.

1 John 4:18 states:

"SUCH LOVE HAS NO FEAR, BECAUSE PERFECT LOVE
EXPELS ALL FEAR. IF WE ARE AFRAID, IT IS FOR FEAR
OF PUNISHMENT, AND THIS SHOWS THAT WE HAVE
NOT FULLY EXPERIENCED HIS PERFECT LOVE."

Soak up God's love and seal it into your very being. Fill your
soul with God's healing balm of peace. Make each day a masterpiece of God's glory: 24 hours of life, drenched in Jesus Christ.

Job 22:21 tells us:

"SUBMIT TO GOD, AND YOU WILL HAVE PEACE;
THEN, THINGS WILL GO WELL FOR YOU."

Let go of your past with the precious blood of Jesus, through His deliverance and forgiveness. Let your soul be permanently cleansed and made spotless. Flourish in His love. Go through every door that God is opening for you, unlocking the treasures of Heaven. Beautifully brilliant is the path that God has for you; focus on it and do not look back. You are never going back again. You are moving forward!

Being Set Free

When we are born again, we are new creations in Christ, but our minds and souls can still be oppressed. The enemy can still try to imprison us with sickness, fear, infirmity, lack, and doubt. However, there is power in the name of Jesus that sets people free from the oppression of darkness.

John 14:12-14 proclaims:

"I TELL YOU THE TRUTH: ANYONE WHO BELIEVES IN ME WILL DO THE SAME WORKS I HAVE DONE, AND EVEN GREATER WORKS, BECAUSE I AM GOING TO BE WITH THE FATHER. YOU CAN ASK FOR ANYTHING IN MY NAME, AND I WILL DO IT, SO THAT THE SON CAN BRING GLORY TO THE FATHER. YES, ASK ME FOR ANYTHING IN MY NAME, AND I WILL DO IT!"

When Jesus went to be with His Father, He sent the Holy Spirit to be with us and in us. Through the Spirit, we have the same power as He did on Earth. This power is even greater, because Jesus is now seated at His Father's right hand, interceding for us!

It says in John 8:32:

"AND YOU WILL KNOW THE TRUTH,
AND THE TRUTH WILL SET YOU FREE."

If we don't know our identity in Christ, which is the truth, how can we experience victory? Only when we undoubtedly know who we are will Satan have zero ability to affect our lives. If you believe in and declare the word of God, the enemy will fear you, and you will never live in bondage again!

When we fear God, we never have to fear anything else, ever. The kingdom of God is inside of us through the power of the Holy Spirit. It is forever expanding to protect, guide, anoint, and continuously bless us. Everything in our soul that is not of Him will be driven out of us. Call on the name of Jesus and be set free!

A Prayer for Personal Revival

Father,

Create in us a notion of divine urgency, a humble and holy discontent, a reverential dissatisfaction with the things of the world. Let it lead us to repentance and personal revival.

We prepare our hearts to fully receive Your Holy activation, bound and sealed in Your unconditional love. We ask You to heal us, soften us, and humble us, so our hearts will be softened and pliable to receive Your redeeming mercy.

We ask for a Godly interruption of our wrong and limited thinking. We welcome Your holy correction and Your perfect peace, to bring us significant growth and unlimited favor.

Holy Spirit, infuse us and consume us with Your grace, truth, and wisdom. Break the routine and the mundane. We wholeheartedly welcome You into our lives with Your strategy to enact change in us. It's time for a glorious revival.

Enlarge us in the land we are about to enter and occupy. Let our minds be steadfast, and in complete harmony with your plan.

Let Your whispers of change be forever etched in the valleys and crevices of our desperately yearning hearts. Breathe restoration in us, through us, and for us! We wholeheartedly glorify You and praise You, sweet Father.

In Jesus' name we pray.

Amen.

"REVIVE ME ACCORDING TO YOUR WORD."

PSALM: 119:25

Living Your Potential

John 10:10 states:

> "...MY PURPOSE IS TO GIVE THEM A RICH
> AND SATISFYING LIFE."

Jesus opened the doorway for us to have eternal life in the kingdom of Heaven. If all we can see is the earthly life we live now, then our expectations will be very limited. But, the Kingdom of God is not far beyond our grasp; it is available, here and now! Jesus died that we could have and enjoy life to the fullest, now. Through Christ, we can reach for our true potential.

Let every decision you make be made with eternity in mind. Sin is an "enjoy now, pay later" plan. The problem with that approach is that we never know when "later" is coming. Eternity is a long time to get it wrong!

Luke 9:60 states:

> "BUT JESUS TOLD HIM, 'LET THE SPIRITUALLY DEAD
> BURY THEIR OWN DEAD! YOUR DUTY IS TO GO AND
> PREACH ABOUT THE KINGDOM OF GOD.'"

Just as strongly as it was present in Jesus two thousand years ago, the Kingdom of God is present today in us. It is at hand! We were born for a time such as this. Hold your beliefs; do not waver, and do not grow weary in doing well. Take a stand, and usher in Jesus, in all His radiant glory!

Philippians 2:13 states:

"FOR GOD IS WORKING IN YOU, GIVING YOU THE DESIRE AND THE POWER TO DO WHAT PLEASES HIM."

Live life without enslavement to this world and its temporary pleasures. Seek God and His Kingdom. Live a life strengthened in faith. Reach your highest potential and, above everything else, believe!

No More Excuses

Isn't an excuse just a little white lie that the enemy tells us to keep us in a state of mediocrity? The Bible is overflowing with excuse-makers, starting off with Eve!

Genesis 3:13 tells us:

> "THEN THE LORD GOD ASKED THE WOMAN, 'WHAT HAVE YOU DONE?' 'THE SERPENT DECEIVED ME,' SHE REPLIED. 'THAT'S WHY I ATE IT.'"

Excuses give us permission to settle for less than God's best. It seems we always have an excuse for our shortcomings. We always have something to blame for our less-than-stellar lot in life. We declare that this is how it always is for us and our families.

We get so caught up in the past that we can't see hope staring at us through the dirty windows of our own self-appointed limitations. We breathe in the status quo and exhale the mundane.

Most failures come from a history of excuses and a lack of perseverance. Closed doors don't always mean that entry is forbidden! Most of the time, they mean that God has another door for us, opening into something bigger and better. We must move forward and keep knocking!

Matthew 7:7 states:

> "KEEP ON ASKING, AND YOU WILL RECEIVE WHAT YOU ASK FOR. KEEP ON SEEKING, AND YOU WILL FIND. KEEP ON KNOCKING, AND THE DOOR WILL BE OPENED TO YOU."

It's time to receive the victory God has in store for you. You can do all things through Christ, who gives you strength! Success will ultimately come to you when your vision becomes bigger than your excuses.

Through Christ, you are made new and made whole in every area of your life! Stop making excuses to not pursue your dreams. Become a new creation in Christ, and let Him free you from your excuses. Let the promises of God settle in your heart. Declare these truths and let them override your excuses, now!

Being a Contender for Christ

Be a Warrior of the Word!

Jude 1:3 states:

> "DEAR FRIENDS, I HAD BEEN EAGERLY PLANNING TO WRITE TO YOU ABOUT THE SALVATION WE ALL SHARE. BUT NOW I FIND THAT I MUST WRITE ABOUT SOMETHING ELSE, URGING YOU TO DEFEND THE FAITH THAT GOD HAS ENTRUSTED ONCE FOR ALL TIME TO HIS HOLY PEOPLE."

Are you a contender in this life? God fights for us every second of every day. The question is, do we fight for Him? When we pray the Lord's Prayer, we ask our Father that His will be done on Earth as it is in Heaven. As Christians, we are called to be contenders. Jesus has given us the ability, the grace, and the power to do what we need to do for the Lord. We need to bring the things of Heaven here to Earth!

We do not have to go around looking for Jesus. Through His death and resurrection, we have the Holy Spirit living in us. Through Christ living in us, He can now be everywhere at once, doing His great works, and using us to contend for His truth.

Leviticus 26:8 gives us this promise:

"FIVE OF YOU WILL CHASE A HUNDRED, AND A HUNDRED OF YOU WILL CHASE TEN THOUSAND! ALL YOUR ENEMIES WILL FALL BENEATH YOUR SWORD."

We are the ambassadors of Christ, His earthly army placed on the battleground that is our world! Even the toughest battles can be fought and won, not with weapons, but on our knees in prayer.

I, for one, want to be a contender. I want to be the eyes, the ears, and the mouthpiece of God. I want to be His hands and feet, a way for Him to do His will here on earth.

Keeping Your Eyes on Jesus

I find myself increasingly shocked when I watch the news, or see the covers of the magazines in the grocery store. Why does it seem that the wicked of this world are prevailing in their evil schemes and living prosperous lives? Why does it appear that people who are not even remotely living for God seem to have it all? The answer is very simple: they don't!

They are living for the here and now, void of all the blessings of Heaven, which can only be acquired through a relationship with Christ.

The time we spend on earth is a mere blink of an eye in comparison to the eternity we will have with our loving Creator and Heavenly Father.

Job 36:17 states:

> "BUT YOU ARE OBSESSED WITH WHETHER THE GODLESS WILL BE JUDGED. DON'T WORRY, JUDGMENT AND JUSTICE WILL BE UPHELD."

We must never be obsessed with the apparent unfairness of these people's so-called successes. We must look at our own lives, stay in repentance, ask for forgiveness, and continuously try to be an example of God's love here on Earth.

We must remember this: If God punished evil immediately, none of us would be here! We all need to be thankful that God gives us renewed chances to repent and return to Him. He gives us an unmerited grace to look at ourselves in revelation. We can see our own sins and steadfastly turn away from them.

Keep your eyes on Jesus! He alone will take you to the magnitude of peace, joy, and brilliance our Father has in store for us!

Not Looking Back

When the people of Israel fled Egypt, running for their lives while followed by all the Pharaoh's men, they wound up on the beach of the Red Sea. Imagine their great fear, the feeling of defeat and complete horror.

However, God pulled off the most mind-blowing miracle! It never entered the minds of the Israelites that, right then and there, God would perform a miracle, that He would part an entire sea for them, and let them cross safely on dry ground! God then swallowed up all of their enemies as the sea was commanded to flow back into its trough. Can you imagine witnessing this astonishing supernatural phenomenon?

Genesis 50:20 states:

> "YOU INTENDED TO HARM ME, BUT GOD INTENDED IT ALL FOR GOOD. HE BROUGHT ME TO THIS POSITION SO I COULD SAVE THE LIVES OF MANY PEOPLE."

Through the blood of Jesus, the enemy has been destroyed under your feet! The miracle is in the trial you face. God is all powerful. He goes before you and uses what the enemy has meant for harm to bring to you a complete victory.

This is how our loving God moves and operates on our behalf! There is nothing that He is not prepared to do for us. There is no rescue mission too hard or too risky for God. You are worth it to Him!

Job 5:9 tells us:

"HE DOES GREAT THINGS TOO MARVELOUS TO UNDERSTAND. HE PERFORMS COUNTLESS MIRACLES."

God is making a way for you. He's clearing a path. Do NOT look back. Through your faith and declaration that God is who He says He is, you will cross your Red Sea, and you will see that you have been planted, safely and freely, on the other side!

A Faith Jesus Marvels At

In all of Scripture, there are only two things that Jesus marveled at, and both concern levels of faith.

Matthew 8:8-10 states:

"BUT THE OFFICER SAID, 'LORD, I AM NOT WORTHY TO HAVE YOU COME INTO MY HOME. JUST SAY THE WORD FROM WHERE YOU ARE, AND MY SERVANT WILL BE HEALED.' [...] WHEN JESUS HEARD THIS, HE MARVELLED. TURNING TO THOSE WHO WERE FOLLOWING HIM, HE SAID, 'I TELL YOU THE TRUTH, I HAVEN'T SEEN FAITH LIKE THIS IN ALL ISRAEL!'"

And Mark 6:4-6 tells us this:

"THEN JESUS TOLD THEM," A PROPHET IS HONORED EVERYWHERE EXCEPT IN HIS OWN HOMETOWN AND AMONG HIS RELATIVES AND HIS OWN FAMILY. "AND BECAUSE OF THEIR UNBELIEF, HE COULDN'T DO ANY MIRACLES AMONG THEM EXCEPT TO PLACE HIS HANDS ON A FEW SICK PEOPLE AND HEAL THEM. AND HE WAS AMAZED AT THEIR UNBELIEF."

A faith that makes Jesus marvel is something worth looking into! The Roman soldier believed that Jesus' word was all that was needed to manifest the miraculous. The scripture from Mark states how the lack of faith disallowed even Jesus from performing miracles.

These opposing degrees of faith show us what we need to bring the miraculous into our lives.

If you can believe in the written Word of God, you are in a place to receive miracles, as Jesus marvels at that kind of faith. Many of us find it hard to believe in things that we cannot physically see or touch, but, if we could see all things, there would be no need for faith.

Many times, we think that if we don't see immediate results, God has not been moved to answer our prayers. But, God's ways are not our ways. His timing is always perfect.

When you're waiting on God, stand and believe. Let Jesus marvel at your faith!

Highway of Holiness

Isaiah 35:8 tells us this:

"AND A GREAT ROAD WILL GO THROUGH THAT ONCE DESERTED LAND. IT WILL BE NAMED THE HIGHWAY OF HOLINESS. EVIL-MINDED PEOPLE WILL NEVER TRAVEL ON IT. IT WILL BE ONLY FOR THOSE WHO WALK IN GOD'S WAYS; FOOLS WILL NEVER WALK THERE."

Doesn't that sound like a highway that we all want to travel? It is always good to check ourselves, and to ask God to reveal to us anything that might grieve the Holy Spirit. If there's any hard-heartedness in my life, I want Him to remove it from me, so that I might travel on this great highway.

Ephesians 4:31-32 states:

"GET RID OF ALL BITTERNESS, RAGE, ANGER, HARSH WORDS, AND SLANDER, AS WELL AS ALL TYPES OF EVIL BEHAVIOR. INSTEAD, BE KIND TO EACH OTHER, TENDERHEARTED, FORGIVING ONE ANOTHER, JUST AS GOD THROUGH CHRIST HAS FORGIVEN YOU."

God knows we are not perfect. He made us in His image, but He also knows the desires of our hearts. We want our hearts always to be pure, right, and good. Let us aim our hearts in the right direction. Let us keep our eyes steadfast, and always looking straight ahead to Him. He is the light and our road to salvation.

This highway is only found by following God. He is making a road for His people to walk in His ways.

Lord, we ask that You guide our steps on Your Highway of Holiness. Let us be surrounded by a mighty hedge of protection, guarded continuously by Your ministering angels. Let Your heavenly warriors highlight the way, and keep us focused on You. Let us stay firm on this mighty road that leads to the abundance of all mercy, grace, love, and sweet joy.

One Word

Jeremiah 23:29 asks:

> "'DOES NOT MY WORD BURN LIKE FIRE?'
> SAYS THE LORD. 'IS IT NOT LIKE A MIGHTY
> HAMMER THAT SMASHES A ROCK TO PIECES?'"

One word. Just one word from God has the power to change everything. He speaks, and the universe is formed. He speaks, and miracles happen. He just says the WORD, and all of Heaven springs into action. Believe in the WORD!

Hebrews 4:12 states:

> "FOR THE WORD OF GOD IS ALIVE AND POWERFUL.
> IT IS SHARPER THAN THE SHARPEST TWO-EDGED
> SWORD, CUTTING BETWEEN SOUL AND SPIRIT,
> BETWEEN JOINT AND MARROW. IT EXPOSES OUR
> INNERMOST THOUGHTS AND DESIRES."

Let the word of God be the strong tower, the pillar, and the fortress where we are hidden from danger.

2 Timothy 3:16-17 tells us:

> "ALL SCRIPTURE IS INSPIRED BY GOD, AND IS USEFUL
> TO TEACH US WHAT IS TRUE, AND TO MAKE US
> REALIZE WHAT IS WRONG IN OUR LIVES. IT CORRECTS
> US WHEN WE ARE WRONG, AND TEACHES US TO DO

WHAT IS RIGHT. GOD USES IT TO PREPARE AND
EQUIP HIS PEOPLE TO DO EVERY GOOD WORK."

The word will prepare and equip us to lay claim to an absolute victory! I pray that we do not shrink into the fear of the unknown, but tread fearlessly on the water. I pray that we grab a hold of the hem of the precious garment of Jesus Christ and never let go. Let us rise up and prepare our feet for the battle. Let us call forth the victory we already know we will win through the powerful word of God!

Do Not Be Deceived

It's time to pray against deception. The Bible tells us that, in the last days, we will be greatly deceived. This is no time to ride the fence and be double-minded. We must get on board with the revival that God is stirring up in each of us. We must decide if we are going to accommodate the world and what happens in it, or if we will refuse to compromise our beliefs and follow the word of God.

Revelations 2:14-16 states:

"BUT I HAVE A FEW COMPLAINTS AGAINST YOU. YOU TOLERATE SOME AMONG YOU WHOSE TEACHING IS LIKE THAT OF BALAAM, WHO SHOWED BALAK HOW TO TRIP UP THE PEOPLE OF ISRAEL. HE TAUGHT THEM TO SIN BY EATING FOOD OFFERED TO IDOLS AND BY COMMITTING SEXUAL SIN. IN A SIMILAR WAY, YOU HAVE SOME NICOLAITANS AMONG YOU WHO FOLLOW THE SAME TEACHING. REPENT OF YOUR SIN, OR I WILL COME TO YOU SUDDENLY AND FIGHT AGAINST THEM WITH THE SWORD OF MY MOUTH."

So many strong Christians back off and fail to declare the truth. We fail to be a witness of the Word. The truth sets people free. Love people, and tell them the truth. It's not God's will that any man should perish. The enemy loves tolerance because tolerance doesn't spread the Gospel.

Revelations 2:13 states:

"I KNOW THAT YOU LIVE IN THE CITY WHERE SATAN HAS HIS THRONE, YET YOU HAVE REMAINED LOYAL TO ME. YOU REFUSED TO DENY ME, EVEN WHEN ANTIPAS, MY FAITHFUL WITNESS, WAS MARTYRED AMONG YOU THERE IN SATAN'S CITY."

We must get a powerful knowledge of the Word and stand firm! TRUST and believe in it! Defend it! Be an advocate, and a mover and shaker of the Word. There is no compromise. Get off the fence and stand, declaring your victory. Do it now, before it's too late!

Blessed to Be a Blessing

1 John 2:15 tells us:

> "DO NOT LOVE THIS WORLD NOR THE THINGS IT
> OFFERS YOU, FOR WHEN YOU LOVE THE WORLD, YOU
> DO NOT HAVE THE LOVE OF THE FATHER IN YOU."

We must be careful not to get caught up in the materialism of this world. We must remember to always seek God and His kingdom, and then everything else will be given unto us.

One thing that money always fails to buy is true peace. Genuine happiness and pure joy come from having a true relationship with our Heavenly Father. We are continually trying to fill the void with possessions, until we let Him fill our longing hearts.

The enemy loves keeping us distracted with the things of this world. Anything that comes before God will keep us on a detour, living a sinful life that is void of blessings and sincere joy. We must be very diligent and stay on guard.

I believe there is a reason God does not give us more than we can handle. I believe we need to grow up in Him, and be mature enough to handle the responsibility that comes with great blessings.

Do we know for certain what it means to give? It is the law of reciprocity: give, and it shall be given unto you.

Malachi 3:10 tells us:

> "'BRING ALL THE TITHES INTO THE STOREHOUSE,
> SO THERE WILL BE ENOUGH FOOD IN MY TEMPLE.
> IF YOU DO,' SAYS THE LORD OF HEAVEN'S ARMIES,

'I WILL OPEN THE WINDOWS OF HEAVEN FOR YOU.
I WILL POUR OUT A BLESSING SO GREAT, YOU WON'T
HAVE ENOUGH ROOM TO TAKE IT IN! TRY IT!
PUT ME TO THE TEST!'"

God blesses us to be a blessing. When your mind is set on helping others and knowing the reasons for your blessings, God will pour prosperity into your life.

The Green Lifesaver

Psalm 138:8 states:

> "THE LORD WILL WORK OUT HIS PLANS FOR MY LIFE—FOR YOUR FAITHFUL LOVE, O LORD, ENDURES FOREVER. DON'T ABANDON ME, FOR YOU MADE ME."

When I was a kid, my grandmother always had a roll of multicolored Lifesavers in her purse to share with us. As great as I thought they were, I still had a problem: When she offered me one, I had to take the next one in line in the roll. I remember closing my eyes and secretly praying against the dreaded green one. "God, please don't let me get a green one. Let my brother get that one!"

Instead, I would hope and pray for orange or — best of all — the shiny, brilliant red cherry one. The absolute jackpot of the Lifesaver world! I laugh, looking back at my heartfelt prayers over Lifesavers, but has much changed?

Life is like a roll of Lifesavers. There are many colors and flavors in our lives, and we must take the good with the bad. Our attitude during the tough times can determine how quickly we get through them. We must stay in peace and keep our joy.

God reminds us that, no matter how many green Lifesavers you have to choke down, the bright red cherry ones are coming. We will always get to those good moments and happy times. Peel the paper back and let God reveal your blessings.

Good times are coming! We live in this world, and, in this world, we will have trouble, but God has not left us. He's preparing the way. He's saying, "Hold on and trust me; the red Lifesaver is next"!

If we never experienced disappointment, how could we fully appreciate our blessings? Have a blessed day! May it be filled with cherry Lifesavers!

Battling the Enemy

Our emphasis has been wrong. Spiritual warfare is not continually engaging in combat with the enemy, who has already been defeated. It is living in the victory of the ONE who has already defeated him! We don't have to live in a battle zone. We can declare ourselves victorious through the word of God and the blood of Jesus. It is finished — we won!

In the desert, Jesus did not put up with the enemy's temptations — and, in our lives, we don't have to, either. Jesus used the power of the spoken Word of God to win the battle and silence the enemy, and we can do the same thing.

The Bible says, in I John 4:17:

> "AND AS WE LIVE IN GOD, OUR LOVE GROWS
> MORE PERFECT. SO WE WILL NOT BE AFRAID ON
> THE DAY OF JUDGMENT, BUT WE CAN FACE HIM
> WITH CONFIDENCE BECAUSE WE LIVE LIKE JESUS
> HERE IN THIS WORLD."

We have that same authority over the enemy. The spoken Word of God is the truth! We have the same power that Jesus did. The enemy is the father of lies, and he is powerless when the blood of Jesus is present.

Acts I:8 states:

> "BUT YOU WILL RECEIVE POWER WHEN THE
> HOLY SPIRIT COMES UPON YOU. AND YOU WILL
> BE MY WITNESSES, TELLING PEOPLE ABOUT ME

EVERYWHERE—IN JERUSALEM, THROUGHOUT JUDEA, IN SAMARIA, AND TO THE ENDS OF THE EARTH."

Take the rugged nails from the cross that Jesus gave up His life on, and let them puncture the enemy's lies and eradicate them. We are fully authorized by the Lord Jesus Christ, and empowered by the Holy Spirit, to speak and act in His name. We can live, move, and have our being in Him! We are to be agents of His kingdom here on earth.

The battle is already won, and the enemy has to flee. Declare victory — speak with the sword of truth!

Do Not Make God Wait on You – Be Obedient

Doesn't it always seem like we're continually waiting on God to do something? We pray and pray some more, and it seems we're just endlessly waiting for Him to make His move.

I feel that many times, He has to wait on us! He has to be patient with us. Often, He has to remove something from us, shape us, move us, and prepare us to be able to handle our purpose in Him.

Deuteronomy 4:1 states:

> "AND NOW, ISRAEL, LISTEN CAREFULLY TO THESE
> DECREES AND REGULATIONS THAT I AM ABOUT
> TO TEACH YOU. OBEY THEM SO THAT YOU MAY LIVE,
> SO YOU MAY ENTER AND OCCUPY THE LAND
> THAT THE LORD, THE GOD OF YOUR ANCESTORS,
> IS GIVING YOU."

He is waiting for our obedience, our complete reliance, and our determined trust.

God is standing there with open arms, ready to pour blessings on us. Yet, we get caught up in the snares of this world, and the aimless sidetracks of the enemy's detours. We bind the very hands of God through our sheer disobedience.

We think we can do everything on our own. We become self-appointed know-it-alls. We lose our trust, we lose our patience, and we fail to surrender our circumstances to God.

Friends, I ask you to search your heart and ask God to reveal how you may have veered off track. What things do you need to lay down on His altar? What do you need to fully surrender to the Lord?

He is so determined to bless you. Do not make God wait on you one more second!

We Will Not Lose a Thing

John 18:8-9 tells us what Jesus said when the Roman soldiers came for Him:

"'I TOLD YOU THAT I AM HE,' JESUS SAID. 'AND SINCE I AM THE ONE YOU WANT, LET THESE OTHERS GO.' HE DID THIS TO FULFILL HIS OWN STATEMENT: 'I DID NOT LOSE A SINGLE ONE OF THOSE YOU HAVE GIVEN ME.'"

We do not have to lose a single one that was given to us, either. We do not have to lose a single one of our children to the secular world. We do not have to lose loved ones to the plans of the enemy. We do not have to lose peace, health, joy, or anything else the Lord has given us.

The next thing that happened in this scripture was Peter leaping forward to take matters into his own hands, as told in John 18:10-11:

"THEN SIMON PETER DREW A SWORD AND SLASHED OFF THE RIGHT EAR OF MALCHUS, THE HIGH PRIEST'S SLAVE. BUT JESUS SAID TO PETER, 'PUT YOUR SWORD BACK INTO ITS SHEATH. SHALL I NOT DRINK FROM THE CUP OF SUFFERING THE FATHER HAS GIVEN ME?'"

How many times do we do that? How many times do we step up and try to do it ourselves? We must get out of our own way, and trust that God's plans are always the best plans. We may have good intentions, but, sometimes, we act abruptly. We lose our peace and our self-control, and then it is "score one for the enemy." If Peter had had his way, Jesus would not have gone to the cross! God's plan for us to be redeemed and restored to Him would have been thwarted!

Trust that God's plan will prevail, and we will not lose a single thing He has in store for us.

Faith Starts Where Logic Fails

John 6:5-9:

> "JESUS SOON SAW A HUGE CROWD OF PEOPLE
> COMING TO LOOK FOR HIM. TURNING TO PHILIP,
> HE ASKED, 'WHERE CAN WE BUY BREAD TO FEED ALL
> THESE PEOPLE?' HE WAS TESTING PHILIP, FOR HE
> ALREADY KNEW WHAT HE WAS GOING TO DO. PHILIP
> REPLIED, 'EVEN IF WE WORKED FOR MONTHS, WE
> WOULDN'T HAVE ENOUGH MONEY TO FEED THEM!'
> THEN ANDREW, SIMON PETER'S BROTHER, SPOKE
> UP. 'THERE'S A YOUNG BOY HERE WITH FIVE BARLEY
> LOAVES AND TWO FISH. BUT, WHAT GOOD IS THAT
> WITH THIS HUGE CROWD?'"

We all know what happened next. There was no logic that enabled the boy's small lunch to feed thousands and thousands of people. It was faith that let everyone eat until they were full — a tangible experience of ending up with more than you started with.

Faith was on display in the active obedience of the disciples. They dared to believe, and stepped out to feed the multitudes. Through their simple act of saying "yes" to something that made zero sense, God was able to work through them and perform a miracle.

Before He can perform a miracle, God first needs the vessel, the believer. He needs the faith. He just needs that simple act of getting into agreement with Him. Just say yes to Him!

Through our obedience and faith in what we cannot see, God will do even more, much more than just enough! God will meet our needs, and then give us abundant leftovers!

What's in your basket? Get your faith out and be audacious for God. You have not because you ask not! Ask big, think huge! God will triumph where logic fails!

A Spirit without Limits

John the Baptist spoke of Jesus, saying in John 3:34:

> "FOR HE IS SENT BY GOD. HE SPEAKS GOD'S WORDS,
> FOR GOD GIVES HIM THE SPIRIT WITHOUT LIMIT."

Do you have any idea what it means, that, through salvation, we are promised the gift of the Holy Spirit, and it is without limits?

The Holy Spirit — the very presence of God — is within us, helping us live as God promised and intended. As believers, we have divine authority. We have V.I.P. access to God as children of the King, and there's nothing He won't do for His children.

Does this not astonish you in every way? We must realize what we have available to us. We must try to grasp the magnitude of the amazing strength and fortitude we have as children of God.

By faith, we can appropriate the Holy Spirit's power every day of our lives! Since Jesus is in us through the power of the Holy Spirit, we already have all the help, qualifications, and provision we will ever need.

When we call on the name of Jesus, all of Heaven's armies come to our rescue. We need not fear anything or anyone.

John 14:21 states:

> "THOSE WHO ACCEPT MY COMMANDMENTS
> AND OBEY THEM ARE THE ONES WHO LOVE ME.
> AND BECAUSE THEY LOVE ME, MY FATHER WILL LOVE
> THEM. AND I WILL LOVE THEM AND REVEAL MYSELF
> TO EACH OF THEM."

Through our obedience, God will give us revelation of what He wants to use us for, and what our purpose is in Him.

Have you received the Spirit of God without limit? If not, then seek the baptism of the Holy Spirit. Today, ask for a fresh outpouring of God's love, and a fresh anointing of your life.

Step by Step

Let God take you along your path, one step at a time.

Psalm 37:23 states:

> "THE LORD DIRECTS THE STEPS OF THE GODLY.
> HE DELIGHTS IN EVERY DETAIL OF THEIR LIVES."

When God acts, He does it in an orderly and specific way. Nothing is haphazard. Each action has been brilliantly planned out. Our world and our universe were created on purpose, and life was spoken into existence, all at the perfect time and in perfect order.

When the children of Israel — all three million of them — were led out of Egypt, they went in orderly ranks. Had they known ahead of time all the hardships that would unfold on their journey, it would have been way too much for them to handle.

God allows us to only see things one step at a time, so we must trust Him. He won't give us things we are not yet ready for. He won't take us too far, too fast. Stay close to God, knowing and understanding that He is already in your tomorrows.

Many times we want what I like to call "Insta-God!" We want Him to just show up and miraculously change our circumstances and fix all of our problems, right now! But, to be in complete obedience to God, we must accept things the way He has ordained them. God often chooses to help us gradually. There are so many lessons to be learned in the valleys. He guides us through lessons that cause us to grow, stretch our faith, and prepare for the blessings to come.

Today, trust that God has put you on the exact step of the road where you are meant to be. We will all be so much stronger, wiser, and blessed as a result of having done things in God's perfect timing and order!

Why Did Lucifer Fall?

Scripture tells us that Lucifer was beautiful, anointed, and had the keys to all the blessings and favor of Heaven. How, and why, did something change so profoundly in him? How did his heart become so hardened to God?

It all started with a desire for self-recognition. Pride and arrogance won in the battle over his mind, and he decided to become his own God. He desired praise; he longed to be worshiped.

Isaiah 14:13-14 tells:

"FOR YOU HAVE SAID IN YOUR HEART: 'I WILL ASCEND INTO HEAVEN, I WILL EXALT MY THRONE ABOVE THE STARS OF GOD; I WILL ALSO SIT ON THE MOUNT OF THE CONGREGATION ON THE FARTHEST SIDES OF THE NORTH; I WILL ASCEND ABOVE THE HEIGHTS OF THE CLOUDS, I WILL BE LIKE THE MOST HIGH.'"

So, with that, he was banished from Heaven, and hurled out of the Kingdom.

Proverbs 16:18:

"PRIDE GOES BEFORE DESTRUCTION,
AND HAUGHTINESS BEFORE A FALL."

He made his choice, and there was no do-over. And now, he wreaks havoc on all mankind. Because of Lucifer's choice, we too are left with choices. There are pathways of both good and evil. There is evil in this world; people are hurt, suffering, and in despair. We need God's wisdom to decipher His plan and His purpose for us.

It is scary to ponder what choices we may want to rethink. We never know the day in which we will be called home. But, we have authority over all evil through the blood of Jesus and His finished work on the cross. The enemy was unleashed to spread evil in the world, but we are ultimately much more powerful because of God, who is in us.

Remember: No matter how bad things look, and what the enemy does to provoke us, God will grant us a promotion. Declare victory, and remember who had the authority to kick whom out of Heaven!

God won then, and God wins now. Receive your victory in Him!

Getting Rid of Your Pride

Pride always goes before a fall!
  Psalm 10:4 states:

> "THE WICKED ARE TOO PROUD TO SEEK GOD.
> THEY SEEM TO THINK THAT GOD IS DEAD."

The very first sin recorded in the Bible, with Adam and Eve, was not murder or lust: it was pride. It was pride that made Eve reach up for the forbidden fruit that promised to make her as knowledgeable as God.

How far are you willing to fall? What are you willing to risk? Is it worth it?

Adam and Eve were living in a utopia. They wanted for nothing. And yet, there was a pull, an attraction to the fruit, and the temptation of their own pride.

What happens between thinking about sin and actually committing a sin? What causes us to choose the wrong fork in the path? We are all sinners by nature, and it is pride that calls us to wander off our paths to victory.

1 Peter 5:6 states:

> "SO HUMBLE YOURSELVES UNDER THE MIGHTY
> POWER OF GOD, AND AT THE RIGHT TIME HE WILL
> LIFT YOU UP IN HONOR."

The enemy prowls around, looking for unguarded hearts and minds that have been letting in the wrong thinking. He unfairly plays his stacked deck, and displays his enticing hand. Through the weakness of pride, we fall victim to the illusion that we are capable of doing everything on our own.

Proverbs 11:2 states:

> "PRIDE LEADS TO DISGRACE, BUT WITH HUMILITY COMES WISDOM."

When you feel that you are being tempted, check your pride at the door. Call on the name of Jesus, and let God's wisdom rule in your heart!

God Is Willing

I believe, sometimes, that we over-think and over-analyze the Bible, when, in reality, its truths are quite simple. We simply need to trust God's word and apply it to our lives every day.

Luke 5:12 states:

"IN ONE OF THE VILLAGES, JESUS MET A MAN WITH AN ADVANCED CASE OF LEPROSY. WHEN THE MAN SAW JESUS, HE BOWED WITH HIS FACE TO THE GROUND, BEGGING TO BE HEALED. "LORD,' HE SAID, 'IF YOU ARE WILLING, YOU CAN HEAL ME AND MAKE ME CLEAN.'"

This man undoubtedly knew that Jesus could heal him, but he just wasn't sure if Jesus wanted to. This simple act of faith so touched Jesus that He touched the man and made him clean.

If you have read anything about leprosy, you know it is an awful, harsh disease. It is incurable and highly contagious; the man would have been covered with painful lesions and scabs. Yet, Jesus was unfazed. He touched the man without hesitation. This was probably the first human touch that the man had felt since he had contracted the disease.

Many of us believe that God would not be willing to do things for us because we've done too many wrong things. This is false. He is always willing to help! We should never doubt His love for us.

Just like the man with leprosy, we must realize that we cannot cure ourselves. We are unable to do such a task. But, we should faithfully and humbly ask for Christ's redeeming help. With one touch or one command, what ails us can end! He is willing to cure us!

Dumping Your Baggage

Here is an uplifting idea! Make today the last day you carry around baggage!

Are you living in shame, guilt, and condemnation? These things are NOT from the Lord. The enemy loves nothing more than to keep you bogged down in your own shame, feeling guilty for past mistakes.

We drag along these piles of baggage that are weighing us down. They are filled with regrets, grudges, anger, bitterness — the list goes on and on. We feel that we need to unpack all this unhappiness every now and then and look it over. Then, we pack it all back up, stuff it down, and make one more burdened trip around the mountain.

Romans 8:2 states:

> "AND BECAUSE YOU BELONG TO HIM, THE POWER OF THE LIFE-GIVING SPIRIT HAS FREED YOU FROM THE POWER OF SIN THAT LEADS TO DEATH."

God is saying, "No more! Drop the baggage — I am all you need!" What the enemy means for harm in your life, God will use for good.

It's time to forgive yourself. It's time to move forward, letting go of what lies behind. Keep your eyes steadfast on Jesus and never look back!

Repent of your past sins, leave them at the foot of the cross, to be covered in the blood of Jesus, and walk away, light as a feather.

Romans 8:1 states:

"SO NOW THERE IS NO CONDEMNATION FOR
THOSE WHO BELONG TO CHRIST JESUS."

Make today the first day of the rest of your life. Make today the day that God comes to set the captives free. Never unpack your baggage again; forgive, be forgiven, and dump it today!

Being a Sharpened Tool for the Lord

Isaiah 10:15 asks:

> "BUT CAN THE AX BOAST GREATER POWER THAN THE PERSON WHO USES IT? IS THE SAW GREATER THAN THE PERSON WHO SAWS? CAN A ROD STRIKE UNLESS A HAND MOVES IT? CAN THE WOODEN CANE WALK BY ITSELF?"

We must always remember that we are just the tools in God's hands. God wants to use us in amazing ways, but we are only useful to the extent that we allow Him to do it.

If we are an ax in the hands of God, we must keep the blade sharpened to be effective. Our knowledge of the Word sharpens the ax, and we are iron-sharpeners for one another. When the blade of an ax becomes dull, it cannot be used for its purpose until it is sharpened again.

All tools do different things. Think about a hammer and a screwdriver: each is the best at doing its own important job. Likewise, If God has given you special talents, you are anointed to do something very specific that God has purposefully planned for you to do. We must never regard our gifts and talents as something of our own creation. Instead, we must know where they come from. We can do nothing without God, just like an ax cannot chop wood without someone who is deliberately and skillfully swinging it.

Romans 9:17 states:

"...I HAVE APPOINTED YOU FOR THE VERY PURPOSE OF DISPLAYING MY POWER IN YOU AND TO SPREAD MY FAME THROUGHOUT THE EARTH."

Be a tool that God can use. Be someone that God's skilled hands, and His supernatural wisdom, can use to glorify His kingdom. Be the one who says "yes" to being used by God!

How Is Your Spiritual Eyesight?

Psalm 119:18 states:

> "OPEN MY EYES TO SEE THE WONDERFUL
> TRUTHS IN YOUR INSTRUCTIONS."

How is your spiritual eyesight? Is your ability limited to only seeing your circumstances in the real world? Are you incapable of seeing the bigger picture? Do you focus on your problems and your lack of abilities to overcome them? Or, do you see how great God is, and His ability to overcome anything?

2 Kings tells the story of when Aram was at war with Israel. The prophet Elisha used his spiritual eyesight literally to keep God's chosen people safe. 2 Kings 6: 9-10 says that, whenever the King of Aram planned to move his army:

> "[...] IMMEDIATELY ELISHA, THE MAN OF GOD,
> WOULD WARN THE KING OF ISRAEL, "DO NOT
> GO NEAR THAT PLACE, FOR THE ARAMEANS ARE
> PLANNING TO MOBILIZE THEIR TROOPS THERE."
> SO THE KING OF ISRAEL WOULD SEND WORD TO THE
> PLACE INDICATED BY THE MAN OF GOD. TIME AND
> AGAIN ELISHA WARNED THE KING, SO THAT
> HE WOULD BE ON THE ALERT THERE."

The king of Aram, learning of this, sent his armies to seize Elisha. Elisha's servant was terrified to see that their city was surrounded. 2 Kings 6:15-17 continues:

"[...] 'OH, SIR, WHAT WILL WE DO NOW?' THE YOUNG MAN CRIED TO ELISHA. 'DON'T BE AFRAID!' ELISHA TOLD HIM. 'FOR THERE ARE MORE ON OUR SIDE THAN ON THEIRS!' THEN ELISHA PRAYED, 'O LORD, OPEN HIS EYES AND LET HIM SEE!' THE LORD OPENED THE YOUNG MAN'S EYES, AND WHEN HE LOOKED UP, HE SAW THAT THE HILLSIDE AROUND ELISHA WAS FILLED WITH HORSES AND CHARIOTS OF FIRE."

With his "spiritual eyes" open, the servant could see that the supernatural army, God's army, the one he couldn't see with his physical eyes, was so much bigger than any army of men.

Through our faith, we can realize that God is doing much more for us than we could ever imagine.

Will you open your spiritual eyes and see the chariots of fire that fight for you whenever you say a prayer? Today, you can watch Jesus win your battles with your eyes wide open!

Do You Have True Salvation?

Beware, and do not get caught up in the snares of this world! Do you have pure heart salvation, or only mind salvation?

Knowing the Bible and quoting scripture does not automatically mean you are a Christian. The enemy himself believes in God and knows scripture!

Loving only those who love you is easy. Even sinners do that! However, have you forgiven the ones who have hurt you the most?

If your salvation has not made you want to become a new creation in Christ, perhaps you need to rededicate your ENTIRE HEART to Jesus.

Philippians 2:12 states:

"DEAR FRIENDS, YOU ALWAYS FOLLOWED MY INSTRUCTIONS WHEN I WAS WITH YOU. AND NOW THAT I AM AWAY, IT IS EVEN MORE IMPORTANT. WORK HARD TO SHOW THE RESULTS OF YOUR SALVATION, OBEYING GOD WITH DEEP REVERENCE AND FEAR."

We should do everything without fault-finding or complaining. We should live clean, blameless lives. We should shine bright, and bring hope to the hopeless.

Know the Word for yourself. But, also rejoice in the Lord, and always seek a relationship with Him. Spend time in His presence, and He will teach you how to safeguard your faith. Seek Him first in all things, and pray against evil and deception.

The secret to a changed life is to repent and submit to God's will. Pray that God gives us the desire and the power to do what is solely pleasing to Him.

Sometimes, we need a check-up for our hearts and souls! God has begun a good work in you. Today, with your entire heart, commit that you will trust Him to bring it to completion.

The Living Water

There are so many wonderful things to be learned from the story of the Samaritan woman who met Jesus at a small well in her village. Jesus was tired from a lengthy walk, and was sitting wearily beside the well. The woman came near to draw water, and He asked her for a drink. The woman was quite shocked that Jesus, being a Jew, would ask a Samaritan woman for a drink, as this was not common practice. Jews and Samaritans did not associate with each other. She asked Him why.

John 4:10 tells us:

> "JESUS REPLIED, 'IF YOU ONLY KNEW THE GIFT GOD HAS FOR YOU AND WHO YOU ARE SPEAKING TO, YOU WOULD ASK ME, AND I WOULD GIVE YOU LIVING WATER.'"

He went on to say in John 4:14:

> "[...] THOSE WHO DRINK THE WATER I GIVE WILL NEVER BE THIRSTY AGAIN. IT BECOMES A FRESH, BUBBLING SPRING WITHIN THEM, GIVING THEM ETERNAL LIFE."

As they talked, she realized that He was the Messiah. She ran back to her village to spread the word, and the villagers listened to her and followed her back to meet Jesus.

What can we learn from this simple encounter, this divine appointment that became part of Biblical history?

Jesus wants to give us everything. His love for us is pure and unconditional. He wants us to be filled with His living water. We are no surprise to Jesus. He knew everything about the Samaritan woman and her checkered past. And yet, He was so kind and patient with her. Even though she had been a sinner, He was right there for her with open arms. She ran to the village to tell everyone about this man because she was changed, and now was used to spread the good news of Jesus.

No matter what we've done, no matter how broken we are, God can use us! God is the fountain of life! The same living water that Jesus promised at the well can quench your thirst forever!

Miracles Are God's Idea

God is calling us to a new level of faith! A powerless gospel was never His intention.

Mark 16:17 states:

"THESE MIRACULOUS SIGNS WILL ACCOMPANY THOSE WHO BELIEVE: THEY WILL CAST OUT DEMONS IN MY NAME, AND THEY WILL SPEAK IN NEW LANGUAGES."

Do we wholeheartedly believe in what we pray? Or are we just saying the words? We can have all the power and authority, and live in absolute expectation that we can do greater work. God Himself, as written in the pages of the Bible, expects us to do just that!

We should never lower our expectations of what God can do. Somewhere along the line, it became safer not to believe in miracles. I am here to tell you that miracles happen every day! I have witnessed miraculous events, such as crippled people standing from wheelchairs and walking, healings, and deliverances. My list is huge. God is still God!

Acts 3:16 states:

"THROUGH FAITH IN THE NAME OF JESUS, THIS MAN WAS HEALED — AND YOU KNOW HOW CRIPPLED HE WAS BEFORE. FAITH IN JESUS' NAME HAS HEALED HIM BEFORE YOUR VERY EYES."

God uses us to perform miracles. The groundwork is already laid. It's about us being the instrument in God's miracles: His mouthpiece, hands, and feet. We need to trust God. We only need to believe in what He has done for us. Miracles have always been God's idea in the first place, not ours! We couldn't come up with these things!

Matthew 10:7-8 tells us:

"GO AND ANNOUNCE TO THEM THAT THE KINGDOM OF HEAVEN IS NEAR. HEAL THE SICK, RAISE THE DEAD, CURE THOSE WITH LEPROSY, AND CAST OUT DEMONS. GIVE AS FREELY AS YOU HAVE RECEIVED!"

Spend time getting to know the Lord. Seek intimacy with Him. He will give you a fresh impartation to be His working vessel here on Earth. God will give you power, if you only believe!

Got Faith?

What does faith in the Lord mean?

Faith is not like a faucet that can be turned on and off at convenient times. God is not someone who stands on the sidelines, to be called on only when we're in trouble. We must always and continuously seek Him, so when the trials do come — and they will — we are prepared for battle!

Psalm 112:6-8 states:

"SUCH PEOPLE WILL NOT BE OVERCOME BY EVIL.
THOSE WHO ARE RIGHTEOUS WILL BE LONG
REMEMBERED. THEY DO NOT FEAR BAD NEWS;
THEY CONFIDENTLY TRUST THE LORD TO CARE FOR
THEM. THEY ARE CONFIDENT AND FEARLESS,
AND CAN FACE THEIR FOES TRIUMPHANTLY."

Does faith mean that we only trust God and all of His glory when everything seems to be going smoothly and we don't have a care in the world? It shouldn't! It is when the going gets tough that our faith should be the strongest!

When the trials come, our faith should be put into purposeful action. This is not the time to run or to fear. It's time to speak the Word, to declare God's glorious promises over our situation!

God's power is not diminished by a turn of events or a set of circumstances! God allows such tests for a purpose. They are a call to trust God and stretch our faith. Trials can be either a firestorm of despair, or a refining fire. The choice is solely up to us!

Live your life by continually basking in God's presence. Humble yourself, and welcome Him into your life, even if it is a mess. God is by our side, and He is always with us. He is our guiding light and loving influence. We are more than conquerors in Christ: He always causes us to be victorious!

Praying Big

Are your prayers big enough? Friends, when you do not know what to do, when you are at a loss, when your entire world seems to have turned upside down, look up! Look towards the Lord, our God. He wants to reveal His glorious plans to you and to give you hope.

Psalm 107:28-30 states:

> "'LORD, HELP!' THEY CRIED IN THEIR TROUBLE,
> AND HE SAVED THEM FROM THEIR DISTRESS.
> HE CALMED THE STORM TO A WHISPER AND STILLED
> THE WAVES. WHAT A BLESSING WAS THAT STILLNESS
> AS HE BROUGHT THEM SAFELY INTO HARBOR!"

No matter what it looks like for you, ask Him what you need to do. Ask Him for His plan, His solution. If any man asks for wisdom, God will give it liberally.

John 14:13-14 tells us:

> "YOU CAN ASK FOR ANYTHING IN MY NAME,
> AND I WILL DO IT, SO THAT THE SON CAN BRING
> GLORY TO THE FATHER. YES, ASK ME FOR ANYTHING
> IN MY NAME, AND I WILL DO IT!"

What are you asking for? If we are asking BIG, and thinking BIG, God will do exceedingly, abundantly more than we ask, so what do we have to be worried about? God's got it!

God is a man of His word. He's ready to answer our prayers, but we first must go to Him, humble ourselves, and ask for His assistance. God can take care of all of our needs, with or without us asking. But, when we ask, we acknowledge that He alone is God. We know that we cannot accomplish things with our own strength. When we try to do it alone, we are trespassing on God's domain.

When we pray, who do we think we're talking to? We are talking to the Creator of the entire universe! God can handle whatever it is you need, today and always.

Giving Up

"Pick ONE!" I overheard a frazzled mother yell in the grocery store. Her two young children were in the candy aisle, loudly debating which bag of candy to buy and share. Each child clutched a bag of candy bars as if it were a life vest in the middle of an ocean. It appeared there was a stalemate. The argument worsened, and both kids burst into tears. Finally, the exasperated mother grabbed the candy from her kids and put it back on the shelf, saying: "Forget it! No one's getting any candy now."

I could not help but laugh to myself. I remember those days well! But, then I got to thinking: How many of us make our own stalemate situation with God when He asks us to do something or lay something down? We often obstinately hold out, plead our case, and hope for God to change His mind. How many of our blessings get put back on the shelf because we are too stubborn to give in?

Isaiah 40:28 states:

"HAVE YOU NEVER HEARD? HAVE YOU NEVER UNDERSTOOD? THE LORD IS THE EVERLASTING GOD, THE CREATOR OF ALL THE EARTH. HE NEVER GROWS WEAK OR WEARY. NO ONE CAN MEASURE THE DEPTHS OF HIS UNDERSTANDING."

He knows what we do not. If we are waiting for God to give in to our understanding of a situation, then we are going to spend the next forty years in the wilderness. I, for one, could not go that long with the same pair of shoes. I'm joking, but it's a scary thought, to be off the path that God has so brilliantly planned for you. We must enter the promised land by trusting that God's plan is the only plan for our lives.

Let's surrender and turn back to the loving arms of our Heavenly Father! Let's trust God, and know that He will make the crooked paths straight if we just stop resisting and let Him.

Endless Blessings

The blessings of the Lord are endless. To get them, we must have faith!

We must always affirm God's strength and not our own. We are given supernatural abilities when we grasp that we are nothing without God. When we get out of our own way and allow God's strength and wisdom to take over, to rescue, redeem, and restore us, miracles happen!

James 4:7 states:

> "SO HUMBLE YOURSELVES BEFORE GOD.
> RESIST THE DEVIL, AND HE WILL FLEE FROM YOU."

God wants us to depend more and more on Him. This requires us to fully trust Him in all things, even when our trials seem beyond comprehension. Even our bleakest days and our saddest hours are no match for God's power!

Romans 12:2 states:

> "DON'T COPY THE BEHAVIOR AND CUSTOMS OF THIS
> WORLD, BUT LET GOD TRANSFORM YOU INTO A NEW
> PERSON BY CHANGING THE WAY YOU THINK. THEN
> YOU WILL LEARN TO KNOW GOD'S WILL FOR YOU,
> WHICH IS GOOD AND PLEASING AND PERFECT."

God's manifested presence allows miracles to occur. Heaven meets Earth, and we are not left the same way we were found. He will give us talent, ability, knowledge, wisdom, and strength. He will bless us with the purest peace and the truest joy.

We must stand for all the promises of God, and know that He is the same God yesterday, today, and forever.

God already knows the outcome. He is the author of our stories. Seek God's face and receive your blessings!

Bold as a Lion

Proverbs 28:1 states:

> "THE WICKED RUN AWAY WHEN NO ONE IS CHASING
> THEM, BUT THE GODLY ARE AS BOLD AS LIONS!"

Be bold as a lion for the Lord! What is God calling you to do? What is He stirring in your heart? Step out and do it! God will not ask you to do something that He has not already equipped you to do, even if you do not recognize that yet. Know that He will take care of all the seemingly impossible details of your God-given mission. No matter how hard it looks to you, it's not too hard for God!

Trust God. Let Him take you by the hand and lead you into your divine purpose in Him. Be bold! What are you putting off? Are you deeming yourself unworthy or unqualified? David was a mere shepherd boy who became a great king. He was bold! He put God up against the giant Goliath, and, together, they defeated him!

1 Peter 3:14 reassures us:

> "BUT, EVEN IF YOU SUFFER FOR DOING
> WHAT IS RIGHT, GOD WILL REWARD YOU FOR IT.
> SO, DON'T WORRY OR BE AFRAID OF THEIR THREATS."

We are called to have no fear of man. God can do what men cannot. God is for you, so who would dare to be against you? Be bold for the Lord!

Do not back down! Being judged by others is not a concern; we only need to be concerned with what God thinks of us.

Lord, we are Your humble servants. We are ready. We chose You. We said YES to Your great commission! We will be bold!

Are You Stuck in a Rut?

Are you stuck? Why aren't your plans succeeding? Why are you not moving forward?

Proverbs 16:1-2 states:

> "WE CAN MAKE OUR OWN PLANS,
> BUT THE LORD GIVES THE RIGHT ANSWER.
> PEOPLE MAY BE PURE IN THEIR OWN EYES,
> BUT THE LORD EXAMINES THEIR MOTIVES."

Do we ever take our motives into consideration? Why do we seek certain things? What drives us?

We may think that we are doing the right thing for the Lord, and that we are pure-hearted before Him. But, before putting any plan into action, we must ask ourselves three very important questions:

1. Is this plan in keeping with God's truth?
2. Will my plan work out in real-life conditions?
3. Is my attitude about my plan pleasing to God?

Proverbs 16:3 goes on to say:

> "COMMIT YOUR ACTIONS TO THE LORD,
> AND YOUR PLANS WILL SUCCEED."

We can come up with good plans and lay the groundwork. If it is in harmony with God's will, and we have sought God's wise counsel FIRST, then, yes, our plans will succeed!

There are distinct ways that we can fail to commit to the Lord. Some people commit superficially; they say that the project is being done for the Lord, but they are really doing it for self-gratification. Others give God only temporary control, then take it back the moment things get rough. They jump ship and blame God. Then, there are those who have a brilliant idea, but put no effort into it, and expect God to do it all for them. God is not a fairy godmother with a magic wand! He expects us to lean on Him, but He also expects us to step out in faith.

We must find the balance. We must trust God, as if everything depended on Him, because it does. Simultaneously, we must be working hard, as if everything depended on us. Do all you can, and God will do all you can't. Get out of that rut!

Taking Authority

Isaiah 55:11 states:

> "IT IS THE SAME WITH MY WORD. I SEND IT OUT,
> AND IT ALWAYS PRODUCES FRUIT. IT WILL
> ACCOMPLISH ALL I WANT IT TO, AND IT WILL
> PROSPER EVERYWHERE I SEND IT."

Do not utter words of defeat; instead, let every word that comes from your mouth be the written Word of God! We are victorious in Him! We can defeat the enemy, and forbid him from trespassing on our lives.

2 Corinthians 4:13 states:

> "BUT WE CONTINUE TO PREACH BECAUSE WE
> HAVE THE SAME KIND OF FAITH THE PSALMIST HAD
> WHEN HE SAID, 'I BELIEVED IN GOD, SO I SPOKE.'"

We must allow the Word of God to continually change us. Let's renew our minds daily, to be like Christ and to believe Him! We get to choose daily which thoughts we will accept and which ones we will deny. Whose word do we believe? We must continually ask ourselves this so we can take every thought captive.

2 Corinthians 4:18 tells us:

> "SO WE DON'T LOOK AT THE TROUBLES WE CAN SEE
> NOW; RATHER, WE FIX OUR GAZE ON THINGS THAT
> CANNOT BE SEEN. FOR THE THINGS WE SEE NOW WILL

SOON BE GONE, BUT THE THINGS
WE CANNOT SEE WILL LAST FOREVER."

God's power to heal, bless, restore, and provide is not changed or diminished by our circumstances. When faced with a need that has already been paid for on the cross, we have an immediate choice to make. Whose word will we believe: the enemy's, or God's?

Take authority! Learn the Word for yourself, ready your feet for battle, and fight the good fight of faith! We can do all things through Christ, because He gives us strength.

Testifying — You Are an Overcomer

Why do people suffer so greatly? Does our suffering serve a purpose that can be beneficial?

Being broken helps us discover who we really are. Our lives are not found in the darkness; darkness doesn't define us. True identity is found after having come through the darkness. God extends His hand of sweet, merciful grace while we are still in the pit of despair. Even there, God is close. He is nearer than our very breath.

God turns all things around for good. If we never experience failure, how do we fully appreciate success? Learn valuable lessons in the trials!

James 1:2 states:

> "DEAR BROTHERS AND SISTERS, WHEN TROUBLES
> OF ANY KIND COME YOUR WAY, CONSIDER
> IT AN OPPORTUNITY FOR GREAT JOY."

Yes, we do get knocked down. We get hurt, angry, and confused. But, those negative feelings are not what define us. After we get through them, they become stories of victory. Ultimately, they are the life stories and testimonies that will cultivate a harvest of blessings. We will get up again! With Jesus, we can and will do all things. Your story matters. Testify!

Revelation 2:7 states:

"...TO EVERYONE WHO IS VICTORIOUS
I WILL GIVE FRUIT FROM THE TREE OF LIFE
IN THE PARADISE OF GOD."

We are overcomers through the blood of the Lamb and the word of our testimony. Speak up! Declare your victory! Speak life into your circumstances. You are a conqueror in Christ!

Conclusion

These entries have always been a foundation of peace and wisdom for me, and I hope they have also become relatable lessons for you. I pray that God will use this book to bring peace and understanding to all who read it. I pray that you will remember certain entries as you walk through life. I hope they uplift your spirit and bring you peace!

I hope these 100 days together have been a source of peaceful and uplifting inspiration for you as you walk with the Lord.

For more inspiration and uplifting content, visit ninaandmichelle.com, and like "Nina Keegan Ministries" on Facebook. You can also search your local television listings and YouTube for *Grace Grace with Nina & Michelle*.

"MAY THE LORD BLESS YOU AND PROTECT YOU.
MAY THE LORD SMILE ON YOU AND BE GRACIOUS
TO YOU. MAY THE LORD SHOW YOU HIS FAVOR
AND GIVE YOU HIS PEACE."

NUMBERS 6:24-26

About the Author

Nina's life radically changed 25 years ago, when Jesus became her Lord and Savior. She has since devoted her life to sharing God's message of hope and victory through the grace of His son, Jesus.

After over 10 years of devotional writing for various ministries, including the Christian Broadcasting Network, Nina Keegan became co-host of the popular Christian television show, *Grace Grace with Nina Keegan and Michelle Humphreys.*

Grace Grace is focused on spreading the Gospel through media of magnitude. The show is featured on television networks across the US, Europe, and Africa. Their ministry financially supports orphanage projects across the globe.

With an audience of over 1,000,000 interactions per month, Nina shares the gospel daily on her popular Facebook devotional page, "Nina Keegan Ministries."

Nina is called to be an End Time harvester for God's Kingdom, and to carry out His will, playing her part in His great commission. It is Nina's hope that, through her ministries and powerful testimonies, people's lives will be forever changed. Nina believes that we are all here to play an important role in the advancement of God's kingdom.

Nina Keegan is the mother of two grown sons and a daughter-in-law. She lives with her husband, Richard, in the Houston Area.

"TO GOD BE ALL GLORY IN ALL THINGS.
APART FROM HIM, WE CAN DO NOTHING."

JOHN 15:5

Made in the USA
Coppell, TX
21 October 2020

40038263R00125